A KNOWN ALCOHOLIC

Four Unique stories each with unexpected twists and endings.

GEORGE M. OKORA

GEORGE OKORA

ISBN: 1718875797

ISBN-13: 978-1718875791

DEDICATION

WE ALL CONFABULATE FROM TIME TO TIME. TO SOME PEOPLE HOWEVER, THEIR CONFABULATIONS ARE A REALITY IN THEIR OWN MINDS. THE COHERENCE OF CHRONIC CONFABULATORS DEPENDS ON THE PLAUSIBILITY OF THEIR STORIES. LIARS SPEND AN INORDINATE AMOUNT OF TIME SUBSTANTIATING THEIR TALES AND LIES MUCH TO THE DETRIMENT OF THE AGREIEVED PARTIES. BEFORE REPEATING INFORMATION THAT IS DAMAGING ABOUT A PERSON ESPECIALLY ONE YOU HAVE NEVER SPENT ENOUGH TIME WITH TO REALLY KNOW WHO THEY TRULY ARE, ASK YOURSELF A FEW QUESTIONS. AM I SPREADING THE MISINFORMATION BECAUSE OF MY OWN INSECURITIES OR FEARS? OR AM I SPREADING THE INFORMATION BECAUSE I HAVE CREDIBLE EVIDENCE TO AGREE WITH THE INFORMATION?.WE ALL NEED TO THINK TWICE ABOUT REPEATING HARMFUL INFORMATION ABOUT PEOPLE. THE DAMAGE YOU DO WILL MAKE YOU AS GUILTY AS THE ONE FROM WHOM YOU HEAR IT. SOMETIMES EVEN IF A PERSON HAS DONE WRONG, WE NEED TO FORGIVE THEM. NO ONE IS PERFECT. WE MAKE MISTAKES, LEARN FROM THEM AND MOVE ON. IT IS FOOLISH TO NAIL SOMEONE TO THE WALL BECAUSE OF ONE GREVIOUS MISTEP WHILE FORGETTING THE NINETY NINE GOOD DEEDS THE PERSON DID.

CONTENTS

A KNOWN ALCOHOLIC

A KNOWN ALCOHOLIC

SHORT STORIES

FOUR UNIQUE AND AMAZING STORIES WITH

UNEXPECTED TWISTS

- ❖ A KNOWN ALCOHOLIC,

- ❖ KENROY,

- ❖ HIS FIRST DAY AT SCHOOL,

- ❖ PRENTICE AND STACY.

1   SECRETS WE KEEP.

"A lie has travelled halfway around the world while the truth is still tying its shoes"...

Winston Churchill (British Prime Minister)

The teenage boy looked back at the swimming pool and saw the teenage girl waving hard at him. The teenage boy waved back to the teenage girl as she waved to him from the public swimming pool. The swimming pool was just below the grounds of the recreational park. "She really must be having a great time in the water because she might dislocate her arm by the way she was waving it" he thought to himself.

He turned back around and headed towards the exit. He went through the lobby for a quick refreshment to replenish his energy before leaving. He had just come from the pool and left a few minutes after two teenage girls entered to swim. He had been there one hour. That was enough for him.

As he sat down to hydrate himself, a piercing scream so shrill that touched the very fiber of his being and probably those who heard it, rent the air. He dropped his bottle of coca cola and rushed towards the direction of the pool. Other patrons followed suit.

They all went down the hill where the pool was located and horror of horrors, they saw the teenage girl's friend that he had earlier waved to distraught and completely hysterical. He did not have to be a mind reader to figure out what had just happened. Intuitively, he threw his glasses off to the side and jumped into the deep end of the pool and in ten seconds had managed to pull the fourteen year old from the deep end. With immediate and accurate precision, he performed CPR on her with chest compressions and all. Despite his best efforts, it was too late. Yvonne as she was called, was pronounced dead by paramedics who had arrived on the scene three minutes later.

They covered her and took her lifeless lithe body away. Her mother had also been contacted and Torrance heard a cry of pain come from the grieving mother that could not be described by the best orator.

Three hours later, Torrance went and bought himself a four packer. He was nineteen and fresh from high school. In his country, eighteen was the legal beer drinking age. He was not drinking to celebrate anything. He was drinking to blur the day's tragic event.

He remembered the screams from the teenage girl and the mother and took a big swig. "What else could probably go wrong today?" He paced back and forth wondering what had just happened earlier that day. "She was happily swimming and waving one moment and eight minutes later she is dead. What happened? "As Torrance pondered the day's events in his mind, he dropped his beer bottle on the carpet." Oh my holy gosh. Yvonne was not waving at me because she was happy. She was waving at me very hard because she was drowning". Never did Torrance know that this unfortunate and sad tragedy could set in motion a string of events that no person in their lives could ever have imagined happening.

The tall man walked over to the juke box and selected one of his favorite tunes. How he was even walking was somehow miraculous given the amount of alcohol that he had consumed. He somehow had a high tolerance level for alcohol and it showed. "Turn up the volume please Mandy" he yelled to the bartender who had seen this before. Sometimes you would stop wondering what could be worse than fingernails scratching a chalkboard when you heard the tall man yell.

Unfortunately that sound made by the nails and board is sweet music compared to what comes next. He remembered the swimming pool. Was he a murderer? By all means no. He could not fathom why a fourteen year old who was one of the best swimmers in her school went down under the water like that. She had seen there before countless times. What happened differently that day was a complete shock and mystery to him. Torrance took another huge swig of his beer. He had never told a soul about this because it was not about him. Two parents had lost their only daughter. Only a fool could go around trying to explain what could have been and other what ifs as if that could bring her back to life.

Torrance had decided to work in the health care industry. It was almost a subconscious response to redemption. One thing he was good at was his attention to detail that bordered on having an almost identic memory. Perhaps so. He never told anyone that the very things they complimented him for were lacking years ago when a fourteen year old child was waving at him and when he needed such skills the most. Most of his close friends had really never gotten to know this details about him. Even after he got a divorce, he still carried this secret with him. People labelled him as being an alcoholic. He could not care less. He was not. When you have lost so much sometimes initially it is normal human nature to resort to pain numbing alternatives. Initially.

Compounded by the fact of previous losses that only he carried in his heart, this alternative looked like the only easy out. Initially. "Let those murmurers and slanderers as well as the flying monkeys and rumor mongers say whatever they want. Let them talk themselves till their tongues fall off". With those thoughts, he raised his glass to Mike and said "to all the gossips " Mike raised his glass and responded in kind.

"May they talk themselves mute"? Of course it was pain speaking through the alcohol but no matter how the situation was, outsiders just saw one thing. Torrance was an alcoholic which may have been plausible but untrue. He worked two jobs and also wrote books so he did more than the very people who shamelessly pointed fingers at him some of whom did not even work.

Torrance however had no time for the back and forth childishness with anyone. "Someone has to be the adult here". His heart went out to those who had lost mothers, fathers, brothers, sisters, uncles, aunts and whatever Kin related blood term that had robbed bereaved family members. Torrance had lost two brothers and both parents but had not even made it to any of the funerals because he had at any given time either a new baby and kids to take care of and was in a foreign country.

He was now divorced but doing everything possible to provide for his young ones. In life, gossipers never take the time to question why people do things they normally do that they never do. All they see is the result of the person trying to cope with losses in ways that may not be the best but they do it anyway. Some people become silent, some people become promiscuous, some people become violent. Some become depressed. As humans, we all have different coping mechanisms. So it is hilariously ignorant and foolish to cherry pick on some people who are using certain coping mechanisms that may seem controversial and run amok with smear campaigns.

The very same people are the ones who want to be comforted when they are going through a rough patch. They could not like it if they got labelled when they were instead seeking comfort.

The Tiffany Dax was the most popular pub in town where acquaintances had turned into relationships and then into marriages. It was the place where all the stresses of life would be drank down and it was also the place where people could clown around and get cheered for it by spectators who could arguably make better clowns than the clown they could be cheering and egging on at any given moment.

It was also the place unfortunately where getting inebriated was encouraged. No one that wanted to drink as long as they were of legal age was turned down.

The Tiffany Dax was the most popular pub in town. It was the place where marriages had been dissolved, it was the place where people regained their senses after seeing what evils being there had brought up in their lives.it was the place where people ended up incarcerated. It was the place where the joys of life were turned into the stresses of life by liquids that went down smoothly but with horrible consequences.

What came next?   It is hilariously ironic that some people will behave like horny sharks that have smelt a drop of blood in the water when they see or hear about a person they know has fallen upon perhaps tough times. Not only that but amazingly, the same people will believe anything they hear that is controversial more readily than anything that is more sublime in regards to persons that may be trying to sputter back to normalcy as defined by societal norms.

Sometimes people just do not care until you start

shucking and jiving. Well, you are not really going to but the concept is that some speech or words that may grab the attention of some people drive home the point that those who spread slander and malicious gossip have no idea the impact of their words to those whom it affects the most.

Some people for some reasons known only to themselves, like to spread malicious gossip in much the same way as sailors on leave spend money. They just cannot stop without bothering about the consequences their speech will bring.

Perhaps it is just human nature. It is as if humans are preprogrammed for drama, slander, malicious gossip and controversy. Our nervous systems have changed from being docile and submissive to fighting perfection. A majority of the human race strive to do what is wrong instead of what is right. Fighting perfection as stated earlier.

If a person who had been naturally cryogenically frozen for a thousand years would somehow be thawed a

Back to life, the person would be amazed at how people have gone from bad to worse. If the restored person were to turn on the television , no matter what channel, and especially the news, he or she could run back to their capsule, have It frozen and with a small note or disclaimer saying "DO NOT /NEVER RESUSCITATE" . Why? Because we as a species have done tremendously well in all spheres of life and even taken men and women to the moon. However we cannot manage simple courtesies among each other. We lie, squabble, cheat, murder, the list is endless.

When defamatory statements are made against a person even when there are truckloads of seemingly valid evidence to corroborate the statements, people should and must always avoid having any preconceived biases against the alleged perpetrator. Sometimes the availability of evidence is a sign of no evidence. That means that all evidence most be thoroughly examined without any preconceived bias.

Humans have always tended to be followers. Humans...or a majority of them........ always tend to follow what is the common trend sometimes loyally and to a tee with no questions asked. It is almost like blind leading the blind metaphorically. How so? Have you individually grown up in a certain way and raised and trained to do things in a certain way before discovering or finding out that despite the best intentions of those who raised you in this certain way had your best intentions at heart, they were not necessarily the best ways?.

It may have been in any sphere of life that you the reader know personally. When Henry Ford invented The Model -T, his invention was met with skepticism. In some instances, It was received with outright disdain and those who did not think much of the contraption stoned it and the more extreme conservatives even threatened to do the same lynch Mr. Ford whom they thought had invented and done something that was p bordering parallels close to heresy.

All that Mr. Ford did was in effect say "Listen here people, I have been thinking about building a car. Your journeys will be shorter and your horses not needed anymore". Humans tend to be followers. There might be a few who may have wanted to hear him out but people at that particular time knew only horses and carriages and saw nothing beyond the horizon.

Today, that same mentality still pervades society. Case in point. A mother or father may receive a phone call from school and hear "your son or daughter is acting up again. S\he cannot keep still. Perhaps you should consider taking him to a specialist". Of course, no parent wants to be told about their child by anyone who was not their when the child was born, was not there when the child had to be taken to the hospital for any ailments or by someone regardless of position, tells them what they think is best for your child.

In European countries for example, such phone calls are very rare. If the same child is taken to a European country, they will call the parents and the nature of the call is cause for excitement. There they have identified such behaviors or actions, in most cases, as not misbehavior indicative of the child having some "issues" but rather a unique trait in twenty percent of the population. It is called "Sensory processing sensitivity" or in a person, they are referred to as highly sensitive people. So after tests based on certain criteria are performed, the child is identified as being highly sensitive and the parents are told of how to deal with this unique trait and surprisingly, the child once thought as hyper or having issues becomes the quietest and well behaved.

For those in some countries who have less than qualified professionals...who through no fault of their own....are clueless, unfortunately convince the parents to take their child to "specialists" who already know what medication they are going to prescribe to the poor unfortunate five, six, seven or teenage child and the child grows up thinking that something is wrong with them. The Author is by no way prescribing any certain course of action for children. Some people, young or old, do have mental disorders that are dealt with by specialized institutions.

The Author is simply advocating being open minded prior to labelling persons based upon what society is used to branding them. Even people in times past used to think The Earth was flat. Being open to new possibilities as well as irrefutable proof changed that. So before you as a parent give medication to your child or take them to enroll in various sports activities to "burn all that energy" so as to calm them down may be doing more harm than good.

Even when your child perhaps gets after school suspension and later you discipline them for "misbehaving" , you have not helped at all and if you think you can "beat the bad out of them" , what you are actually doing is magnifying the very behaviors that you are trying to eliminate. This is in the case of highly sensitive children. This might sound like a new concept but it is not. Highly sensitive people or kids are simply under advertised. They are not fully understood worldwide. Sometimes unfortunately, people are automatically inclined to label imbibers of alcohol as alcoholics. While this is how It is usually viewed, sometimes the "alcoholic" in question detests drinking the very liquid that has earned them that dubious distinction.

It is like a woman trying to explain that the family car has problems or she had a horrible day at work or that she is tired. The man will say "take the car to the garage, take a day off from work and take a nap". Objectively, the husband has provided the solutions but subjectively, he has not taken the time to look beyond what is being said.

He may not fully understand that sexes do not solve problems the same way. His wife may have probably not cared a smidget about the car or work completely. She just wanted to have the man take her by the hand, seat her down and listen to her cries.

If not, he will probably be sleeping on the couch....by himself...that night.

So is it with many other similar situations. Before we label people and ruin reputations, we have to really look at the bigger picture. Even if the person has done something that is backed by evidence, people should really look past surface illusions. But no, humanity unfortunately is almost hard wired for controversy. They go by what they know. They are used to the "we love our horses and don't want a c-a-r mentality ".

They may even be like the husband who has all the right solutions in the world for any situation that calls for it but not a single answer to the real situation of substance that his wife really wants to hear.

Sometimes people honestly need to reexamine what they hear before they repeat it. Ask yourself these questions prior to labelling a person or pigeonholing them accordingly to the locker in the Locker room of societal ills. Do I have the real facts? Why did the person do what he did? And "Should I believe everything I hear or believe?"

Sometimes there may be exculpatory evidence that

people may miss and by the time you find out that you were part and parcel of a big misunderstanding, you may have caused the innocent party irreparable damage and loss and realization of this will haunt you forever. Not to worry. Imperfect human beings have come a long way. Sometimes we all need readjustment. We are accustomed to shoot first ask questions later but in light of new evidence, we are civil enough to make redactions.

The tall man walked back to his seat and started lip synching the song he had selected. He had been at the bar from the time it opened at ten o'clock in the morning. It was now six in the evening. He had enough drink in him to be legally over inebriated. He somehow knew how to hold his liquor. It was rare that he ever physically manifested his true inebriated state.

"Hallo Mike" said the tall man to the man who walked inside the bar. It was another equally drunk like him and they were both friends in crime as far as drinking was concerned. They could probably both drink any bar dry if they really wanted. It was probably because of the business that they brought any drinking establishment were they welcomed.

"What's new Torrance? Did you hear about what happened to old Sam? ". John shook his head in indifference. "What happened? Mike told his drinking buddy all about another frequent bar client. This was the way it was in the life of this man who drank not because he liked the taste. He had a deep dark secret that he never revealed to many other people. Not even the man seated next to him that preferred to as his best friend.

Some people display pervasive patterns on honesty whenever they are caught with their hands in the cookie jar. They may even end up saying the broken record cliché question like " could you repeat that question" when the question was audibly and clearly asked in regard to falsehoods they may have uttered and why in the first place. They simply malfunction verbally.

No matter how carefully you choose your words, they will always end up being twisted by another. Believing that you can find happiness in a person is an illusion. True, they may make you happy and there have been many cases of people being together as good friends or as marriage mates and being happy. These are facts. Good for them. No doubt they deserve each other and the resulting happiness.

It came through hard work and dedication and commitment. However they did it is between them. On the other hand, there are some people who make each other unhappy. If it was true that happiness is found in people, relationships could be happier and firmly knit. There are some people who are stuck emotionally in what is called a state of arrested development. Such people only care about themselves and what makes them happy in however that term means to them.

They only reflect on how they can manipulate people into fulfilling their personal agendas even if it means lying and spreading slander about a perceived nemesis. It is sometimes funny how certain people you may have taken for friends and up being the forerunners in spreading malicious slander and lies about you yet this are the very same people you could have done anything for.

Sometimes it is true that words can cause more damage than a good old fashioned caning or whipping. Words have the power to bring down great monarchs, destroy reputations, destroy friendships and even make one lose their kids, property or dwellings. Words, especially slanderous words, hurt more than the whip or cane.

It was once thought that the blue gem humanity lives in was flat. This is common knowledge. It was once thought that the earth was being held in place by three or four huge elephants standing on the back of a turtle supporting the earth. That is also common knowledge depending on one's interest in history.

Life is funny. During the days that people were actually convinced it was flat, you could be branded a heretic if you tried to say that the earth was round or any shape other than flat. Some scientists in what was then called the age of enlightenment, used telescopes that clearly showed the roundness of the heavenly bodies as being circular. Even then, the cynics and critics argued that the telescope was pointing skywards and not towards them.

Today, if any sane or reasoning person were to say that the earth is flat, they could wish they were back in the times where it was better being branded a heretic accused of not knowing the shape of the rock they stand on. You may be forced....you will be forced into a strait jacket today if you zealously claimed a flat earth theory and certified as a psychotic, delusional grade A psychopath.

So what is it about humanity that makes generations shift their prevailing mindsets? Is it possible that we still make the same mistakes unknowingly? Today many movie stars, great athletes or even great entrepreneurs are held in such high esteem by the masses and whatever they say is law. Unfortunately, when their aura of invincibility cracks, we get to see that such persons are as human as the rest of humanity with problems as bad as or lives as good as the masses that seem to almost worship him.

The common thread in the past and present is that people have this craving to go along with what is popular. You may as well argue that humanity has consistently played follow the leader. Such patterns and trends unfortunately still prevail amongst present generations. People still believe what they always are told. It is hilariously funny that humanity seems to be programmed to get excitable by negative things.

Even the media gets higher ratings broadcasting negative issues. The moment they broadcast positive things and avoid topics like war, famine, violence and immoral sex, the ratings will drive the particular station and the show it broadcasts into obsoleting or oblivion

Given such facts, is it then not arguable that sometimes what we may hear may be false? We easily get excited when we hear negative things about people and are quick to believe them without thinking twice about questioning the authenticity of validity of what we may be hearing. Unfortunately, some people are quick to spread malicious slander about a person without knowing the damage they may be contributing to. In effect, they are fanning the flames of an already raging inferno and by the time they realize that they have caused unimaginable damage, they cannot do anything about it.

A person may be getting slandered by another and for some strange reasons, some people are quick to repeat the falsehoods they are being told about. Sometimes a person may make a serious mistake. We all do. That may be a single incident yet murmurers and rumor mongers will make a mountain out of a molehill.

They will rarely take the opportunity to apologize when they realize that in effect they were like the driver of the getaway car who did not know that his friends just wanted to go into a bank wearing masks and did not question why. After all, they were just waiting to drive away. If his friends wanted to go inside a bank in disguises and carrying seemingly toy pistols, it has nothing to do with him. That is how it is with people who believe and spread negative talk about others.

It cheers empty souls and it adds life to otherwise full social functions. In some cultures it is seen as a societal menace while in some it is hailed as being chic or even fashionable. However it may be viewed, humanity has been entertained by drink in all its varying forms. Some ancient cultures called it liquid fire and some people have been labelled in terms related to the negative side of this liquid. This liquid had broken homes, separated children from their parents and it has in extreme cases been used against innocent parents to forcefully take children away from them.

We have at one or more times had the pleasure or displeasure, opportunity or regret of meeting a person(s) in a variation of settings. It could be either at a school function, it could be at a fundraising to raise money for either an upcoming funeral for a now deceased patent, brother, sister, aunt , uncle, school friend or whoever it is that we held dear before the cruel hand of death reared its ugly head and robbed the planet of another loved soul. During such occasions, happy or sad, do you notice something about certain people or perhaps just one particular individual?

It is not the gossip who will tarnish the reputation of anyone and everyone they can think of who may have called them out on their despicable behavior and loud mouth and now here they are breathing brimstone and hail fire in return with the hope of managing to convince others to come onboard with them and share the same hate fest.

The expression that is mostly used is "getting a bad vibe" This is common knowledge. We have all used this expression at one time or the other. At school, at work or even when having to deal with the cashier at a restaurant or cafe or at the supermarket. The offending party does not need to say anything. Even their body language may not betray them. No. It is the vibe. It is that feeling you get.

Even law enforcement officials may preemptively use lethal force sometimes because they sensed the offender about to do something that may have led the latter to do something that could put their lives in danger. What however are this "vibes" that you feel with some people? Everyone had their own special version as to the answer they will give. In some instances, a girl and aspiring future bride will bring home a very charming handsome, drop dead hunk of a guy to meet the parents. Dad may say that "She finally brought home a winner and brag to his friends about his soon to be future son in law while the mother may get bad vibes about him and discourage further courtship until they get to really know this "hunk" a little better.

They called him strange. They called him secretive. Some also called him a drunk. They never however questioned the love he had for his children. So strong was the bond that Torrance Steven Taylor have for his children that in some circles it was rumored that he had to make up in love what he lacked in his name. It was a very strange name or a permutation of names put together that Torrance himself wondered if his parents came up with it in a do or dare challenge his parents were involved in and they ended up losing the bet.

Going back fourteen years was different in Torrance's life. Torrance was tall, dark, lanky and fairly handsome. He got the stares from the other sex all the time and thankfully he was not the promiscuous type otherwise his name could not be the only thing he could have to worry about.

He had just finished high school and by all standards was an academic wonder kind. To him it was simply just another day at school each time he went there. He was the captain of the track team and when one laid eyes on him initially, one may not be blamed for thinking that he may have bribed his way to the helm.

He was bone thin, six foot three and had this emaciated looking frame. He could easily pass for a stoner. His demeanor did not do him any justice either. He looked unhinged and totally devoid of any discernible emotion. Even during track meets, the visitors at first saw him on the track and wondered if perhaps he was substituting for the school mascot. It never got any better if the track meet fell on the first of April as it did once.

The other competitors thought it was a prank from their hosts. Here was this tall reedy looking teenager surrounded by storky and well chiseled athletes who in comparison looked vibrant, full of energy and were in all aspects there to win. They could get accolades from the girls and other athletes and when autographs were taken, this tall kind loner was always in the background and invisible.

No one wanted anything to do with a person who looked and acted like frozen fire. Many people have differing views on the beginning of life. Some believe in a creator, some in a big bang or something along those lines while some welcome evolution. Whatever ones vintage is, one thing may have run through many people's minds upon first meeting with Torrance. For the evolutionists, it was argued that evolution may have taken a step backwards with him specifically.

"On your marks, set go!" With that, the gunman fired his into the air for the commencement of the run of the year. It was the national high school athletics championship and Torrance Steven Taylor was the underdog in a race that featured the two time defending champion, the three time record holder who had already raced with some of the best that the world had to offer and then there were a few others in the who is who of school athletes. Then there was Torrance. He did not remember if his name was even announced. This was going to be the run of his life.

He had trained for it and had developed a thick skin through all those years of cat calls and name calling that he endured throughout the last three years of high school. It was only those he had raced with who after racing with him once, never looked down on him...Ever! His ruse was up.

They knew he was the most brilliant visionary in the track. It was rumored that deliberately made himself look haggard and deathly pale to disarm the suspicions of the competition. If he was a military general, Napoleon Bonaparte and even Alexander the great could be impressed with his strategy. At the end of his previous races, one fact was always evidently clear. He was not evolution's leftover.

The fourteen runners took off. The huge television screens showed the runners in all their dazzling arrays of sports regalia. There were University scouts on the stadium all seated at the

Front rows with bags of goodies for the athletes. They came bearing scholarships, job offers, bank accounts, cars and even houses. Small tokens compared to the Kitty they expected from the future bounties they could make from this young men.

Torrance was like a boy among men in this race. He was representing his school district and was the undefeated champion. He never really had any threatening competition. In some races, the competition just were letting him win by default. No one liked getting humiliated in front of a crowd. The athletes got off to a very fast paced start. Torrance knew this tactic. He may well have written the book. He called it the rocket booster thrust. It had always caught the unprepared with their pants down.

Like rockets going to space, they carry three or four pods with enough energy to get them off the ground and it is impressive watching the huge rockets launch off and the ground shaking from the enormous amount of thrust so strong it is felt in fifty mile radius. This goes on for about two minutes as the boosters take the bird way out there into space where once they have done their job of putting the rocket in a safe zone, they are discarded into space like a jilted husband after the wife has used him and seeing no further need for him, dumped him.

The pace was intense. By the third lap, two were caught with their pants down. They were like big fish in a small pond wherever they came from. This was a shark infested ocean and despite the veneer of civility, the sharks were circling each other waiting for a drop of blood. Torrance had raced with those two. Mama's boys he labelled them. It came as no surprise that they dropped out. They were here for the accolades and name recognition. He had beaten them twice in their own school Arena.in front

By the sixth lap, another two had dropped out. Only nine men and boys were left. They were all running at world setting paces. This was not even about the goodies anymore. This was a pissing contest. Mine is bigger so to speak. The young athletes knew that in the next laps, those that were left were to be taken seriously. The stadium roared with adulation and cheering as the school districts egged on their athletes. The big money schools had bought enough stadium space to flee not only their athletic prowess but to show they were not chump change. They were here to win and humiliate.

The next five laps came and went with an athlete going with each. There were only four laps remaining and this is when Torrance took out everything in his arsenal of experience he had acquired over the last three and a half years. Here he was running with the best. Three high school record holders, one national defending champion and then him. No one was even taking him seriously even when he had come this far. "The pale rider representing Hillsboro" as the local editions had dubbed him. Then the most horrible thing happened. With three laps to go, the established competitors threw diapers and pampers at Torrance in a show of disgust because to them, he was a nobody from nowhere who dared challenge their kings.

Torrance had been expecting something like this but not this. This was his baptism and coming of age. He knew that he had touched nerves and nibbled away at the heart of this pompous overrated schools. He was tall, took long strides and looking at him, he was hungry. The look of determination on his face unnerved his competition. His T-shirt came untucked as he increased his pace as they approached the last lap. It was only three of them now. He was not taking anything for chance. He remembered the day he first joined high school. A quiet lad with huge glasses and a knack for books. He was unassuming and when he showed up for track the first week, the seniors laughed at him and pointed at a fictitious direction saying " Nerd club is that a way". After their first race together, he pointed fictitiously in a direction while staring at them saying " jerk class is that a way ". They never imagined he could trail blaze his way to victory.

The bell signaling the final lap rang. This was it. The diapers and Pampers and catcalls and names echo chambered in the arena. Torrance had a tactic that he had used well and that brought him here. When a rocket has used up its boosters, it discards them. Why use them if it does not need to. With Torrance, he used only enough of his boosters to take him through the races. While everyone competing had exhausted theirs with a lap or two to go, that is when he deployed his. And deploy he did. He was in third place and there was a twenty feet gap between the two champions in front of him. They were literally at each other's throats shoving and pushing with no bother about Torrance.

That was their mistake. Underestimating him.

When it was half a lap remaining, the entire stadium went mad. The two overzealous egotistical champions thought it was all for them and so they should. But today even the staunchest critics and hired hooligans all put down their weapons of malice and watched history unfolding right in front of their eyes.

Even the scouts and the stadium sweepers alike as well as stadium security momentarily forgot why they were there. The stoners may even have gone on speed dial to their drug dealers to ask if they had more of the good stuff. They could not believe how Torrance was running.

Torrance Steven Taylor pushed himself and with each stride he took, the other two took two. He seemed to be flying low. The twenty feet became neck to neck with half a lap to go. The two tried their dirty tricks of shoving but in vain. Torrance had put five feet between them.

He had done his homework. He was running, as he found out later, at three seconds faster than any human being in recorded history for this event. When he had put one hundred yards between the two soon to be former champions, he used up his last remaining booster and the pace he was running at was blistering enough to put a nearby ambulance on standby just for him.

Former and current Olympic champions called to speak to him. Some may have thought he was on drugs because human beings do not run like this including the best that ever run. It was said by some on the front bench that when he ran past them, the wind followed and blew down their cups and any woman sitting there was wise not to have put on a loose skirt. Some wondered why he was running like this with fifth yards to go. The world record was about to be shattered. The collegiate record was also about to be history. The indoor, outdoor or whatever other record in this event were all about to be rewritten. Torrance Steven Taylor put his hands up in triumph as he took the ribbon of victory in front if a seventy thousand capacity filled adulating crowd that brought together friend and foe alike. He had learnt one thing about the human spirit that day and it was to serve him in his future.

Man is born free but walks in chains. These are great but false sentiments. The man who coined them may have had his reasons for saying so and we cannot completely understand him or validate or invalidate his sentiments unless we sat down with him so that he could fully explain himself. That however is highly unlikely unless we build a time machine and go back to the time he was still alive at which point someone should tell you to avoid science fiction and stick to reality.

Like all humans who may experience hardships, he may have experienced tough times in his life and sat down, perhaps looked at the stars, the beautiful seas, the birds the trees and even the fish in the ocean. He may have looked at the animals on land and the way they were designed and then looked at humanity. He may have looked at the way women were beautifully created or the way man was handsomely built regardless of imperfections. He may have then looked at the constant bickering going on among his fellow human beings and then wondered why they bicker among themselves.

Are we born in chains? Take a newspaper, any newspaper and turn the pages. It does not matter what location of this orb we occupy and what daily that you are reading. You could be in Nairobi or you could be in Boston or New Delhi. There will always be material that would make you not want to look at any human being the same way. We often attribute certain behaviors to animals but sometimes by comparing our actions to those of wild beasts, it may be hard to draw a line as to who the beasts are if the power of speech was not part of the criterion we used to separate the species.

The papers and all other media are perhaps the only gossip meals that are consistent with the muck that they churn. Some of the stories you read about can turn good milk sour. Think of the worst deeds that human beings can do to each other and they are in the news. Then look at the universe around you. You can see why the author penned this words.

Other than that, many people would say that we were born perfect and free but because of two bad apples, we are now in chains. Sentiment is good. For example, a young woman may receive a beautiful necklace from her parents and if by some unfortunate occurrence, loses her parents, the necklace still remains with her as a reminder of the lobe her parents had for her and she will always sentimentally hold on to it.

There is nothing wrong with this scenario. Sad as it may be or evoke memories of wonderful times past, such are the fatalities of life. Fatalities, not realities. Everyone wants or wishes they could get inside a time machine and perhaps go back to the times when they still had their loved ones. So much so that even Hollywood has produced motion pictures of such thoughts and fictitiously brought them back to life. This is because humans anywhere all have that need to be happy and go as far as creating fictitious realities to momentarily get away from their own.

Let us all stop there for a moment and reexamine our deep thoughts. Why do we wish to bring back times and instances of circumstances that were better or good? Why, some even wish they could go back to the fourth grade or fifth grade and spend one more day with the boy or girl they befriended because they miss the times they had with such people before perhaps they had to move away because their parents got transferred or got a new assignment in a different part of the country or globe as is the case of military families. The common denominator in all situations is that they missed their parents or friends because of the good times that they shared together. This is perfectly okay.

Human beings are designed to naturally want to have good times and memories. So much so that some revert to alcohol or drugs so that they can escape the reality that they exist in. Sometimes however, some wounds are so deep that they are carried forward in adulthood.

Sometimes however, there are some within the human ranks who not only thrive around such painful realities. They feel no compassion to those who suffer and the only thing they may actually be thinking is "thank goodness it is not me". No human can be a judge over the other when it comes to pointing fingers.

None of us can look at another and say "I could never do that" in reference to perhaps some despicable act that was committed by another human. That shows a lack of understanding regarding the evil that man is capable of. This is not to say that we are all evil. Some of us try to keep doing good yet because of our imperfect nature, some slip and do things that they know better than they should have done. They regret what they did and take steps to make amends.

There however are some people who are heartless. Just simply heartless. They will take another person's weakness and turn it into a rumor fest. Someone may have accidentally drank and did something stupid but they took corrective measures to redeem or correct their shortcoming. Say

They may have started programs to educate others of the follies of following the course they took but that does little to assuage the rumor mongers. It is not to say that what they did was anything good. Not at all. However, sometimes we need to look at ourselves before we point fingers at others. We need to make sure that we have taken the log out of our eye before we speak about the twig in another's eye. It could be a variety of mistakes that we make then someone else start a smear campaign about what the person did.

What is even worse are those who repeat the gossip without the entire facts or details of what they heard. It goes back to the reading of the papers. We may read of information that may be true or untrue. So if we get repelled by some things that we may read about, why don't we also get repelled by some of the things that we are told before we decide to repeat them? It seems that humans are attracted by negativity. They would rather repeat I information about a person that can destroy reputations rather than the good that the person had done.

The person may have done one hundred good deeds and committed one bad one but people will prefer to focus on the one bad deed I instead of the hundred. It is a sad fact of life but that happens. We should be careful when listening to slander and damaging gossip and even if a person erred, we should not make mountains out of molehills. No one is perfect. We all fall short sometimes.

Greg as they nicknamed him hard a deep dark secret that hounded and haunted him wherever he went. It was a part of him and despite the glories as people to society seed glory it brought him, it almost wrecked him. The newly crowned champion took the trophy and put his school and school district on the map. It is amazing how his victory had a domino effect for because of him, the district produced champions for six consecutive years after him.

No one in the stadium noticed the extraordinarily beautiful woman in Bulgari shades on one of the nosebleed sections. She could not care less if money was pouring down from the sky into the stadium resulting in a free for all frenzy. No dear. She was here for the main prize and he could keep the trophy and prizes he won. She had come for the main prize.

"Lap it up my sweet" she thought to herself. " You are one in a billion literally who do not even know what they really are" " Lap it up real good because your victorious glory you are receiving right now isn't nothing compared to what you are capable of in that fantastic mind of yours". Seven billion nine hundred and ninety nine hundred million to go. The attractive lady walked out of the stadium. Torrance Steven possessed a talent that he himself never knew he had.

"In the second lane is the first year man from Washington State, Torrance Taylor". The thunderous applause and standing ovation that followed the announcement sent a clear message to the crowd. This was the yearly national track collegiate championships and the crème de LA crème of track stars in the continental United States colleges and Universities were gathered here for a four day slugfest that could see the greats possibly dethroned and the rookies crowned as kings and queens.

The stakes were high and Torrance was not taking chances. He had earned a Fulbright Scholarship to this prestigious University and he had earned his way to become the school Captain. His teammates did not care about his freshman status.

This was a future hall of famer in the making. It was just a matter of time. Torrance stooped slightly as did the other athletes. This was his domain. Unlike the other races, it was customary for the starters to stoop for the mile and other long distance races. "On your marks............ Torrance was used to this. He waited for the gunshot and off he went. He was doing the heats. A total of twenty four started the rave and only eight were needed for the next two heats.

Torrance was confident of securing a spot among the eight. He however was not a big fish in a small pond anymore. He was swimming with the great whites. They was pushing and shoving and even spiking in this event. Torrance knew this and he came prepared. His trainer had advised him never to become caught in a small crowd of runners. It was a grim fact that there were rumors of pre-race conspiracies where some of the athletes were there for recognition only and as such they had no problem targeting threats like Torrance.

All they had to do was flail around and "accidentally" hit his ribs because the ribs protect the lungs and a punctured lung spells the end of a great career. Then if that happened they could target the shin with a well-timed back kick. Torrance had been told about some of the notorious athletes and even shown gruesome and gory videos of his event that made him wonder if this was an auditioning for a Steven King movie or a civilized race among the futures leaders. One thing was for sure. There was not a shred of civility in the videos he saw and quite frankly Torrance wondered how they allowed the culprits to compete even after there was factual evidence as to the presence of this pretentious murderers masquerading as athletes. There was no escalatory evidence to the contrary. The race was in the fifth lap and three had dropped out already. The blistering pace was beyond some of their race standards. "Idiots" thought Torrance. "That is why they are the national championships".

They were better off out instead of taking up space among the other athletes. The athletes came up on the tenth lap. Surprisingly, no one else had dropped out. They meant business. No one was backing out for anyone and even Torrance himself was not going to take any chances. This were future greats.

Just the fact that they were all here was proof enough that they were champions in themselves. Any victories they secured were just confirmations of the fact.

Torrance had to act fast. He was not going to mingle with this crowd that was trying to disable him so he pulled back and just ran on the wings of those in front of him. He tail gated them up until the last lap when convinced that they thought he was not a threat, lunged forward and catapulted himself to romp to victory. This however were just the heats. One more stood on the way before the main course was served. That was what he was more focused on.

Without much pomp and pageantry, the heats for this race were done for the day. It was three thirty in the afternoon and the other heats for the five thousand merits had already been ran. What needed to happen now was four Torrance to get some rest. The organizers had hired out ten hotels for the athletes. They had only hired them but all expenses were going to be met by each respective school. Torrance made his way out of the massive stadium. This stadium had produced greats that were now idolized internationally. This was the best venue for the games to take place because of the psychology involved. When the current crop of athletes ran here, it motivated them to aspire to become like their predecessors. Torrance certainly was inspired to become like the greats. If they could do it, so could he. Torrance had met a young beautiful and talented athlete back in the library lounge at school. He was the one who had made the first move with the "I am new here, could you show me where the checkout counter is" line.

The woman, Nancy laughed almost mockingly but without any malice. "Do you guys still use that line? I thought we left it in the caveman era" He laughed and she showed him what he wanted to find out not because she knew he could not eventually find it but because she wanted to get to know more about this tall young man whose picture she had seen in the schools weekly edition with the headline in the sports column that read "Death is coming to school" with the sub title" make way for the pale rider".

She was the assistant captain of the women's track team and by international standards, a powerhouse in her own right. So Nancy admired the pale rider's athletic resume and could not believe that the lanky tall and handsome yet soft spoken man and unassuming man right in front of her was the best athlete in the long distances and thee best thing to happen to the sports world since the invention of electricity. Yet here he was and she loved the fact about him even more that he was not in tow with an entourage of minions and flying monkeys that usually stroke the massive over inflated egos of other good athletes just to be known as buddies with them. "I am Torrance. My friends call me Greg" Nancy decided to play her cards well. "Nancy, nice to meet you Torrance". She hoped to take off the "or" one day.

They went to the checkout counter and after checking out their books, they walked out together and all the while engaging in small chit chat. Nancy was the poster child of femininity. She walked gracefully and exuded confidence that really excited and attracted men. Torrance told her which dormitory he stayed at and she likewise reciprocated. They agreed to talk later as Nancy was about to go for an evening class later that evening. "Thank you Nancy. Thank you for showing me around the library" said Torrance

"No my dear. THANK YOU"

"This is much better than watching you from the nose bleeds sweetie". She put on her classy Bulgari shades and went to her dormitory room. At thirty eight years old, she effortlessly looked like an eighteen year old.

"Why do they keep sending me to these people?" the grumpy middle aged man asked himself. They are like everyone else and really don't even know that they are uniquely different" The man felt like an underpaid baby sitter.

The huge Boeing jet touched down at the La Guardia international airport at three forty four in the afternoon. The medium height, slightly stocking and well-groomed gentleman alighted from the big bird and looked around. It was almost Summer time and the weather was fabulous. "I could get used to this he thought. He had never been to New York and had only read about it in books and watched it on television. This to him was much better in person than reading about it or watching it on television.

After going through customs, he connected with an Uber that took him to his hotel. While on the way there, he looked inside the cab and was impressed. This was light years away from the horror stories he had heard about as regards cab drivers. They were thought to be rude, arrogant, condescending and sometimes reeking of cheap liquor or beer. That with the stale and choking cigarette breath made any ride around the New York Burroughs a riding nightmare. There were rumors that some riders were willing to forfeit their small fortune in cab fare and prefer to walk. At least that way, they ended up arriving at their destinations alive, a little healthier thanks to the trek and of sound mind. The umber was in every comparison criteria a limousine fit for a king.

The silver Nissan Maxima pulled up by the front entrance of his hotel. A bellhop came and took his luggage as a very attractive usher came and escorted him up the red carpet covered steps of his ritzy hotel. "We have been expecting you Mr. Harrison". Said the lady in red professionally adorned skirt and blouse suit. She had endless legs and the way she walked made any model look childish and uncoordinated in comparison. This was a woman whose bosses knew why she was the perfect fit for the job. "The powers that bed that sent me here are really serious about this mission" he thought as an equally white gloved waiter dressed in the cleanest white he had ever seen offered him a complimentary glass of wine which he gladly accepted. It had been a long flight. This could come in handy.

He opened the door to his hotel suite and the lady in red had to politely nudge him to get inside as he was briefly frozen in sheer disbelief at the enclosure in front of house eyes. "Will there be anything else Sir" the Lady asked. He looked at her name tag and emblazoned in gold was the name "Katya" "Thank you but no Katya. I think I will be okay"

With those parting words the head concierge turned around and left their guest to his own devices. She loved her job and enjoyed meeting people from all continents stop by and she learnt so much about different cultures in the time she had been there. Mr. Harrison took off his shoes and slid into the slippers provided by the hotel. They were very comfortable and the jet lag began to take its toll on him."

I will shower later "he thought to himself as he lay on top of the covers. He could have to shower later because he was too exhausted to even go take a warm shower. Right before he closed his eyes, he opened the file he had taken out labelled confidential and looked at the subject's picture nicknamed the pale rider. "We are going to have the ride of our lives young man"

Mr. Harrison shut his eyes and went off to dreamland

Torrance woke up and went to the bathroom and took a long shower. He reflected on his past and where he had come from. He had grown up the third in a family of four and at the age of seven had lost both his parents to a drunk driver. He recalled the night when he had anxiously awaited his parents to come home so that he could tell them about his day at school.

It had been one of those days where Murphy's Law had paid him a visit. It was a Wednesday morning and as usual, nothing significant had yet happened. He had woken up, showered and prepared for school and kissed his mother goodbye as he took the school bus to school. On the way to school, the bus blew a tire and a replacement was sent to pick up the now fired up juveniles as their behavior showed. It was a free for all debacle inside that bus. There was screaming, name calling, pea shooting and yelling at the top of lungs.

Torrance sat down quietly as was his nature. When the other bus came to pick them up, it was two periods into the school day. Less class today they may have thought. There was one new girl in the bus who took out her shaded prescription Bulgari glasses and heaved a sigh of relief when they finally got to school. "Thank goodness. One more minute with these delinquents and I will go crazy'"

At school, the teacher had taken ill and so it was an empty class all day as even the substitutes were unavailable. Torrance had a presentation to make and so it came as a relief to know that he could ask his father to help him polish up his final presentation for another day.

The funeral procession snaked its way from their house to the cemetery. Torrance was dressed in a black suit and was so diminutive that when he looked up at the adults, all he saw were this sad and mournful looking faces that were lovingly and consolingly worried about him. Relatives and friends he never knew he had all comforted him and he knew that he was welcome to their homes anytime he wanted. He did not fully grasp what was happening. "Are they okay under there" he asked his grandmother who tactfully replied " Yes sweetie, they are indeed okay under there " "Well grandma, tell mommy that I feel like eating rice and her favorite beef stew so am sorry if I was being a bad boy. You can tell them it is okay now. They can come out now"

Torrance sat down on his bed and turned on the television to the sports channel. He watched reruns of collegiate championships from previous years and in his event, there was a male athlete who had dominated the event for the last three years. He was good but nothing in comparison to Torrance. He was nicknamed greased lightning and looking at him race, Torrance could think of no other Moniker befitting him. Greased lightning was a senior and had been in one of the heats yesterday. He had qualified for the finals which were going to be held the next day and it was rumored that Torrance was the underdog who was about to dethrone him, rumors that he had not taken so well

"So you are the pale rider sonny boy" he had said to Torrance earlier in the week when the two first met in the changing rooms. "I guess so" said Torrance nonchalantly. Everything Torrance did was well calculated.

Any hint on his part about his achievements had to be downplayed tactfully. The last thing he wanted was a confrontation with the three time world collegiate champion in his college prime. That was a fleeting moment for Torrance. He hoped it could be the last. Torrance observed the strengths and weaknesses of his major opponent. He jotted them down and later went through them with his school coach.

"This guy always pulls a rabbit out of the hat when we least expect" said the coach. He added "Tomorrow is probably going to be the most memorable and challenging day of your track career Torrance. Bruce Gallagher knows he is going to the pros and the last thing he needs is a superstar freshman humiliating him in the last race of his college career'". Those were not ideal words. Greg had competed with persons like Bruce before and since they knew they had everything to lose, they could do everything possible to leave their legacies intact.

There was a knock on his door. "Come in Nancy ". Nancy had come to take Torrance to breakfast and was looking stunning in a two piece blue sequined outfit that complemented her well-manicured nails and professionally styled hair. One of the perks that came from being the crème of the crop. Torrance was mesmerized yet humbled by her presence. He did not have a history with the females because he had never taken the time to make the history. "You look stunning. I hope you do not break any craning necks out there" he said. A young woman like Nancy was a keeper. He was not the jealous type. He knew that men would stare and stare more at this beautiful specimen. He was okay with that. Matter of fact, it was a compliment to him. He led her out of the door, hand in hand. He himself was dressed immaculately in brand new black dress pants and a blue collar shirt. He was not going to embarrass this beauty by dressing any less attractive.

Torrance had planned a surprise breakfast and so when he took her past the cafeteria that had been set for visiting students, she was naturally surprised. "You know you do not have to do the library line again Greg. We are talking already". He laughed and said that it was not the idea." You told me you love surprises and so let me indulge you dear girl. She looked at him and nodded. They walked past the huge ten foot double doors and made their way to the parking lot where he opened the door for her and waited for her to get in before going around to the driver's side and got in himself. He put the gear on drive and drove ever so cautiously to the rendezvous he had carefully selected.

The car pulled up to a fancy dining restaurant that was well known for being a four star retreat for the rich and famous. He recalled the conversation he had heard earlier yesterday evening with the maître while trying to secure a reservation for this moment. "We have no immediate vacant tables Mr....... Taylor. Torrance Taylor. The Maître d had no clue who she was talking to and fortunately at that particular moment, her immediate Supervisor walked by and politely beckoned to have the phone.

No way were they going to soil their sterling reputation

because the brand new hostess with the most impeccable credentials had not been told about the text messages that are usually sent to the most prominent athletes whenever there is a sports meet. She knew by experience about one basketball college player years ago who had been turned away from this establishment and went on to become a regular at one of their toughest competitor's restaurants. He also went on to become a six time NBA MVP as well as lead his team to a similar amount of rings on the fingers.

No way was history going to repeat itself. Not with a future sports athlete about to have similar titles as the one that got away. No Sir. Not on her watch. "Mr. Taylor I presume, Torrance Taylor" she said. "Yes, that would be correct". "We had a cancellation and we would be glad to accommodate you. I assume it is a table for four".

Experience and training had taught her to start at four with the athletes because they always double dated. 'No, just two thank you kindly" replied the voice on the other end. Two would be fine for her. In the next few years she reckoned, this two could end up bringing teams with even deeper pockets to her establishment. "Very good Mr. Taylor. We shall be eagerly and happily awaiting your arrival. Good day Sir ".

Greg reciprocated the greeting and ushered Nancy into the dining area. They sat down at a booth that had been selected just for them. This was the perfect image of exception that could not get any better or worse for that matter. "Torrance, what is your favorite color? "Green.

Small talk set the evening off and then it was time to go deep. Nancy asked Greg what he wanted out of his life. Greg answered all her questions as frankly and as honestly as he could. He just wanted an opportunity to be like the great that run before him and bring out the best in people. Nancy likewise also wanted to bring out the best in others and seated next to her wax the catch of the century. "This catch has no idea what or who he really is"

The breakfast was absolutely delightful. A fledgling friendship was slowly being cemented in ways that could change the history of the way people see things. However, people only see things the way they have been raised to see things. Any deviation from the norm is either suspect and avoided or is frowned upon. How was Nancy going to make Greg realize his true potential? The bill was settled and the two twenty year olds got up from their table and walked outside to a car that had just been freshly cleaned. This restaurant took its reputation seriously.

The two soon found themselves back at the school

gymnasium at ten o'clock. It was more a calorie burning than workout session. All this time Nancy observed Torrance training and using his athletic prowess to do things that most people with the same body would find almost impossible to pull off. They spoke at length about their families and Nancy was amazed the good relationship that Torrance had with his siblings and parents. Nancy was also curious as to why he was the only one that was talented in being very athletic. She knew of other families like his where there would be even twelve or more children and only one or two were capable of being talented in arts, writing, sports or in one particular area whilst the remaining ones had no clearly defined path in life.

Nancy was falling in love for her friend but it was unethical. It was one of the reasons she always kept her distance from people like Torrance. She probably had no idea what love was until she met Stephen twelve years ago. It was funny that no one ever suspected that Nancy was twenty nine years old but would easily pass for an eighteen year old. " Most people in this planet are like me and have no clue as to why they seem to effortlessly maintain a youthfulness in body and complexion while others seem to age as is normal" she thought. Nancy wanted to let people know about their possible potential and probably make this planet a better place to stay.

Stephen and Nancy were both eighteen years old. The man she would meet twelve years later and still be both twenty year olds have not yet been born. That man as the future would bring out was called Torrance Taylor.

Stephen loved Nancy so much and they had planned to get married when they both completed college. That was to be in the next three or four years. Stephen was a good student and his teachers loved him and respected him as a person. He was good in book writing and had been encouraged to fully exploit his natural abilities even when he doubted himself at times. Nancy was very supportive of him in whatever he loved to do and he likewise was very supportive of her. It was like a match made in Paradise.

So intense was Nancy's love for Stephen she wondered if she would ever feel the way she felt for Stephen with or for any other man. "Perhaps it is teenage infatuation and a temporary good feeling". Time however proved her wrong. The bond she developed with Stephen was so strong that their love as people saw, was almost a fantasy. Nancy and Stephen became pregnant with two twins. A boy and a girl. What more happiness and joy could a couple ask for? By the time the two lovebirds were twenty five, they had formed their own book writing company and written many books about everything and anything. There was however something strange about Nancy that began to make even some of her previous roommates start asking some nagging questions. Nancy was the same as far as her looks were concerned. She simply did not age like everyone else. She was almost twenty five and looked like she was seventeen. Most queries from people ended up in silent resignations of jealousy or despair as most onlookers ended up not trying to argue with Mother Nature. Nancy herself had no idea why she maintained her youthful looks. At least not at that particular moment. She welcomed the looks and thanked her genetics. Stranger than the looks was her seeming ability to bring out the best or the worst in people. She would stand near a person either once or over a long period of time and for some strange reason, the person began to behave in ways that were usually not his or her normal retinue of behavior.

Later on, it was always the same explanation from the person as to their actions. "I am so sorry Nancy, I do not know what got over me". Call it a blessing or a curse but around people like Nancy, there was no deception that the most brilliant deceiver would hide. Nancy had the ability to make anyone show who they really were inside. It was not magic or some kind of hypnosis. No. It was like the three blind men who were asked to explain about an elephant.

One was at the belly and the other was by the trunk while the other was by the ears. So it was the same thing they were explaining but in the way they literally felt. Nancy would be explained in different ways and at the end of it all, it was explaining about Nancy. The other unique ability she had was the ability to take or feel other people's emotions as though they were her very own. If she met someone who was sad or grieving, she would feel like she was sad or grieving as well. If someone was happy. Nancy automatically became happy and remained so for a few minutes even after leaving the vicinity of the person. In the most extreme cases, she would even feel the migraine that someone else felt. It was like transference of energy. Nothing was wrong with her.

She was not some kind of special being or made in a way different from others. She was just different. In all fairness, Nancy was like everyone else. She would empathize, she would be exuberant when it called for it and she felt the pain of others like it was her own. So what was uniquely special about this? Nancy felt this very emotions everyone feels on a way much higher level than most did. There was more.

When she went to a shopping mall or a supermarket, she would not stay there too long. It was too overwhelming for her to go among a crowd of people and transmute all their emotion from them like a dry sponge dipped in a basin of water. It was too overwhelm in. She also was sensitive to the light. Some people are sensitive to light but in the case of Nancy, that sensitivity was magnified. The common everyday light bulb to her became like the sun emitting its rays. So she would always have a pair of sunglasses handy. She had a soft spot for Bulgari glasses as they were manufactured especially to cater to people like her. The highly sensitives.

"Honey, it's been a while since we did anything together. Let's go to for a small two day vacation just you and me. We can leave Ashley and Brad with their aunty Martha. You know how she enjoys having them around" We had a two day vacation two weeks ago baby" came the reply.

2   TRAGEDIES

At the end of it all, Nancy had it her way. Sometimes it was difficult talking to this woman or saying no to her especially if you were her husband. A vacation she requested, a vacation she got. Nancy made the arrangements for the excursion and Stephen did not mind at all where she wanted to go as long as they were both together. The rendezvous location was a cabin on the outskirts of the city center and they were to drop off the kids at Stephen's mother's sister's house on their way there.

"Fatal car accident snuffs the life of three. Survivor in critical condition" That was the headline in one major newspaper while variations of the accident were on other dailies as well. Nancy and Stephen never made it to their destination and never would ever again. The loss of two children yet so young was so devastating to even those who read the newspapers.

Condolences came streaming in from all corners of the country, flowers were sent and donations to help assist the financial undertakings and funeral arrangements were sent. More painful than losing the kids was hoping that the death of the kids was swift. Nancy had lost the three most important things in her life. She mourned her children and best friend. It seemed as though nothing else really mattered.

Nothing was important anymore. She took some personal time away from work and sought some help from her therapist on how to cope with such tragedies such as the one she just went through that happens unfortunately to many persons worldwide. Nancy wished she would die. It would be better if she died with them. It seemed unfair to her that the kids had to die before her. Such thoughts rushed through her mind, consuming her and weakening her. She was losing so much weight that at times, it seemed as though she may need an intervention. However, this was, according to her therapist, normal human response to a tragedy of such proportions. It would have been scarier if Nancy would not have reacted this way at all. She may have but perhaps with her, this was the way she responded to tragedy. She was twenty three when this happened. The first two years were the roughest and toughest for her. As the third year began, she slowly started to come out of her room and actually speak to people. They understood her plight and were supportive of her. It was baby steps. Men would think twice about gestures of friendship. Nancy's wounds were too deep it would take more time before her fractured heart would welcome any man back in.

"Thank you dear for being such a good friend to me" said Nancy to Greg. It was late afternoon on a sunny Tuesday afternoon and the two had gone on a picnic to get away from the hustle and bustle that was the school life where it seemed they were like bees in a nest. Torrance was stroking Nancy's long hair and telling her tales about what he liked about her.

For some strange reason, Torrance brought out in her the ability to trust again. When around him, she was able to bring out pains that were still tucked neatly away from eight years ago that she had decided to keep tucked away.

She opened up to Torrance without necessarily having to tell him what horrors lay beneath. Torrance never hovered. He loved Nancy and trusted her and everything she said. Listening to her was a blessing. So here were twenty year olds bonding together as most people their age did. Nancy would tell that there was something different about Torrance and he had some unique inward strengths that he was unaware of that only Nancy would see in him. "He is a real diamond that is waiting to be discovered and he does not even know it" One thing she noticed about him was the almost extraordinary strength and talent he had when running with the other competitors.

They were all talented in their own right but Torrance took talent to a whole different level. "A highly sensitive who does not realize his true identity". What a waste. Torrance knew he had abilities that others did not have but he naturally assumed it was genetically or something liked that. "Baby, what plans do you have this evening?" Torrance asked his best friend. "I will have to call you later dear and let you know". Nancy promised not to keep him waiting for the reply.

She saw Stephen in Torrance but had to be true to Torrance and herself. It would not be fair on Torrance or herself if she lived with Stephen's memory through Torrance.

No. This was real. The love she had for this young man was genuine. It was a relationship built on honesty, truth and with the main ingredient, love.

"Baby, I will be free after five this afternoon. What did you have in mind?" Torrance had a surprise in store for Nancy and did not tell her. "It is a surprise Nancy. I will let you know. Is seven thirty okay?

One of the reasons that attracted Nancy to Torrance was the way he consistently surprised her with gifts and treats as well as excursions to different places.

The burly man woke up from his slumber and felt like a brand new man after the long flight. He had been given a three month time window to research and gather data about his next target. A one Torrance Taylor. People like Torrance were rare jewels. It was all the same with persons like him initially. They never knew who they really were and what they were really capable of. It was his responsibility to earn the trust of such people and tap their potential for their own sake. So far, he had read the local reports about Torrance and from all possible accounts, Torrance was going to be an easy catch.

However, the burly man was not stupid. He was balanced. He made the same inference with a different target five years ago and things went south. It was an experience he never wanted to re-experience ever again. He called for a taxi and they set off for their destination.

It was the University. Finding Torrance was not going to be difficult. He had hacked the target's schedule and a confidante kept him abreast of Torrance's route, daily habits and also eating habits. The cab pulled up by the University Centre and the passenger got off and tipped the driver. He tucked his newspaper under his left arm and strode into the University commons, the main student lounge at the University center. Then he waited. It was ten thirty in the morning. In twenty five minutes, a tall lanky student would be walking to his favorite student restaurant where he would order a ham and cheese sandwich with a small milk to go with it. Then he would sit down at his favorite booth by himself and munch away on his delicacy. At ten fifty, the scenario materialized and Torrance sat down in front of a burly man reading the latest stock exchange proceedings. He looked pensively at this barely legal young man and said to himself "What a waste". Here was this talented young man who is on his way to making history as the best athlete in his specialty and yet he does not even know what other great abilities that he has. What a waste! The young man in front of him sat down and savored his food. The Canadians were very patient just as the French when it came to eating food.

They ate to enjoy food and not to get full. At least not only to get full. Torrance noticed that he had been lately attracting the ladies and also all kinds of people towards him. At first he thought that it was because of his running talent and subsequent fame that went with it. However, he noticed that once during a school excursion to one of the boondocks, he seemed to attract the same kind of attention even when he had his sunglasses on. There was something strangely odd about all this.

He thought it might be pure coincidence but after the same thing happening countless of times, it was time to look beyond coincidence. He could not exactly put his finger on it so he just let it be what it was. Whatever it was. Torrance also noticed that sometimes strangers would come up to him and suddenly tell him stories about their entire life without him asking them. He would even be in a restaurant eating when out of the blue even the waiters and waitresses would suddenly spill the beans on their marriages, friends as well as relatives. Perhaps people just want to vent and what a better way to do it than with total and complete strangers.

"May I join you please" requested the medium height burly man to Torrance. Torrance saw no immediate sign of danger in this man. The only threat he saw was the amount of bacon that the man had put on his plate. That was another of Torrance's strengths. The ability to observe in detail the nature of his surroundings. He thought that everyone else had that ability but he was wrong. Not many people had that ability. But how could he tell? He did not know how everyone else felt.

The man introduced himself as a freelance journalist who was compiling a report on gifted athletes and he had been assigned to do a story on Torrance and he knew that this was going to be a best seller. Torrance had met a few people like him but his curiosity was aroused by this one in particular. This one seemed nonchalant and unhinged unlike the others he had come across in the past. The others took their assignments passionately. The gentleman sited in front of him could care less about the story. He probably cared more about his bacon being extra crispy. "So what do you want to know exactly Mr.......?" I would like to know what...... ". Mr. Harris. " As I was saying, I would like to know what makes you so driven to consistently win race after race without any seeming effort on your part " If Torrance had a dollar for each time he had this question, he would have been a millionaire many times over. "Well, I better get used to this" he figured.

Tomorrow there would be another bacon eating buffoon asking the same question and so he may as well just deal with it. "I used to love running when I was a little boy. I think it became like an obsession for me. I became passionate about watching athletes compete and decided that I would try to be like them". The burly man jotted down these details. "It has been said that you hardly break a sweat when running. What gives? Torrance looked at the bacon lover and replied "When I know the answer to that question, you will know the answer to that question". With that, Torrance politely and respectfully asked to be excused from the table. Before he did that however, he gladly gave the man his number. There was something about this man that was different and Torrance was determined to find out exactly what it was.

He took his empty tray back to the restaurant and placed it with the other used trays. He thanked his favorite cashiers and thanked the cook once again for a splendid meal. Torrance hurried to his dormitory room so that he could call Nancy and check up on her. He called her line but no one was picking it up. It was a free day due to one of the public holidays and so it was everybody's lazy day. The talented athlete could not find anything useful to do and so just turned on the television.

"Fatal car crash snuffs the life out of blossoming athlete" The news anchor sadly reported the story of a thirty two year old college student by the name of Nancy who was involved in a horrific car accident and was pronounced dead on arrival at the hospital. At first he was curious until they mentioned her age that made him turn off the television station. Miles away, a fat burly man kept the television on to hear more about this tragedy that affected him more than it affected Torrance.

Nancy had gone to the grocery store to buy some ingredients that she was going to use to prepare a meal that evening for her and Torrance. When Torrance found this out, he did not eat anything for fourteen evenings.

Torrance was now twenty two years into his college and athletic career. He had lost so many races to an extent that he lost his academic scholarship. He did not know what was real or false anymore. How could he not even have suspected about the age of this beautiful woman? Not that it mattered to him.

They were both adults and if she was afraid of their age difference, he knew deep down in his heart that they could have still loved each other. Torrance completed his education and took the next flight home. He was not interested in being reminded about events that would torment him and staying here was a sure way of betraying his heart.

At the airport, Torrance looked around one last time. All the dreams, hopes and aspirations that he had for both himself and the love of his life trickled down to a bad memory not because of what he felt was innocent deception but because of what he felt was unfulfilled realities. On a windy September evening, a twenty two year old one time champion on the half marathon boarded a plane back home to Canada. A burly bacon loving man was there at the airport to make sure that he actually left.

The plane landed in Ontario at around seven thirty in the evening. Torrance was back home and awaiting him was his mother and father. The drive home was exciting as a mother and a father were physically seeing their son after four years of him being away from them. Nancy was not mentioned even once. Not during the drive home at least. Torrance's parents had spoken to her a few times before things had gotten serious between their son and this equally talented girl and even after the fact. Torrance took it upon himself to take a one week break from life. He went fishing, canoeing and also mountain climbing. It helped him significantly in coping with the death of Nancy. He had not met Nancy's parents because according to Nancy, they had passed away when she was in her mid-teens. Her family life was one tragedy after another.

Torrance got a job as a school teacher about eighteen days later. He enjoyed teaching middle school and he doubled as the athletics director. He enjoyed his role very much and was such an inspiration to the kids in lieu of his international fame that he had acquired over the past four years. The kids also saw him as a mentor in all that he did. He epitomized triumph in the face of loss. The kids always sent him condolence cards in the mail and sometimes a few offered their sisters or mothers too him as a token of understanding.

He very much appreciated all these gestures and they tremendously helped in him getting back to emotional normally

He was four months into his teaching job when memories of Nancy started flooding back in. He remembered some of the words that Nancy had told him. "Torrance, life is too short. Do not waste it on regrets or on what ifs. Live it out to the fullest".

Those words were like an echo chamber to Torrance. They egged him on whenever he felt like giving up on himself. He just would not give up easily. There were times he thought it was the end of the road for him but he always mustered the courage to keep himself moving. He would not give up on what life had in store for him. He had made a promise to himself and to Nancy and he was going to push forward on that promise.

"Dad, I want to go abroad and continue with higher education ". His mother was out grocery shopping and so for now, dad was the perfect one to tell his future ambitions to. "That is a very big undertaking son. Are you quite ready for such a life again? You barely made it back in one piece the last time and who is to say what you will experience the next time. Are you absolutely certain and sure about this? "I am sure Dad and thank you for the confidence that you and mom have always had in me over the years. "Those are plans that are possibly one or two years away or sooner depending on the circumstances" added Torrance. "Where is it that you want to go to son?" asked the elder Taylor

Torrance wanted to go back to France but it was too sad. In the end, he decided to go to the United States where his cousin Paul was and had already been for the last six years. "Torrance my dear son, you know that we can easily start a business right here in Canada and one day you can take it over". His father was simply doing what all fathers do and that was wishing the best for their children.

Children do grow up and become independent human beings but in the eyes of their parents, they will always be children. The offer was tempting to Torrance. He had not been as close to his parents geographically as he was always away on sporting events all over the country and sometimes they took days off work on end and when he would come back, he had barely anytime to spend with his own friends leave alone his parents. Torrance was not one hundred percent himself. He was a highly sensitive person, a unique breed of humans of whom only one fifth of the Earth's population was. Many people on Earth tend to be naturally sensitive. It is not due to natural selection as one person in the past theorized. No. This was dealing or dealt more with the sensitivities of human beings and unbeknownst to him, Torrance was hit right smack in his genetically bullseye with a slightly more advanced version of it.

His now deceased and to have been wife Nancy was one such person and she had been doing research on Torrance but in the process his natural passions were too overwhelming for her and her heart....and those of other humans for that matter, were like mush when around him. The reason that he was so good in sports was his ability to take on the energies of people around him and retain them within himself without even knowing. So he winning races was really a combined effort and no irony here. The scary thing about all this is that not even Torrance himself knew. Usually such humans who may see this gift as either a blessing or a curse do not even know they have such a trait inside of them. Nancy had gone through a very traumatic event with the loss of Stephen and through her tribulations and distresses, she dug deep down and instead of finding hopelessness, she found a strength that she knew she never heard. T

With this strength she found that she aged slower than most people and when it came to alcoholic beverages, she craved them so bad that people like her become labelled as alcoholics. The actual reason for this is because in the case of highly sensitive people, they tend to have an iron deficiency that is somehow linked to growth and they can get iron from liver, meat, wine, spinach and beer. In some places, lifestyles may vary and some people may not have the time to have a well-made dinner and unknowingly, they find themselves drifting off and indulging by a manner that is quick and easy.

Some of these highly sensitives become like sharks that for days have not had a meal and the first bottle of beer or alcoholic drink is the drop of blood that gets spilled in their ocean of sensitivity. They will always crave it. That is also why and even unknowingly from time immemorial, people have always been advised to eat before drinking. When asked why, they say that one should not drink on an empty stomach which is a logical reason. However, if a person is a highly sensitive, if the meal contains iron rich foods, they will usually find themselves less inclined to head out to the nearest watering hole. Some however are seen by society as alcoholics and said to even have a disease called alcoholism. In some cases, there are medical reasons for such indulgences.

In some highly sensitive people, it is a trait that is genetically passed on down through the ages and it is always the ingredient that the body craves that makes the person seem like they are over indulging. The highly sensitive person also has a craving for red meat more than or higher than usual. It is usually those who are unaware of the trait they have that become the most reckless. Torrance Taylor had too much on his mind one evening and decided to take a sip of wine and top it off with a bottle of beer. It tasted so good and he felt a sudden rush in his body that was euphoric. "I would get used to this" he' said to himself. It was about three weeks before his departure to the United States of America.

Torrance would be mistaken for somebody on vacation during those three last weeks that he was in Canada before departing. His mother cautioned him against such indulgences but it would be like telling a snake not to be a snake. It was a plead to futility. Torrance was not an alcoholic He had just introduced into his system a new substance that was supplement rich in what it craved. The nutrient Iron.

Torrance had started down a path that would take him to places that he did not want to go to. Torrance also discovered that he loved helping people especially those who were less fortunate than him. He decided that he was going to become a nurse or a healthcare professional when he got to America. Torrance found that he also noticed how people felt. When they were sad, it was as if he was the one who was sad. When they were happy, it was as if he was the one who was happy. He also noticed that he had no tolerance for people who indulged in small talk. He was changing into a different person but did not really know it.

Torrance arrived in the United States on December eighteenth two thousand and ten. It was cold and windy and the cold Chicago air was not his cup of tea. He was not used to this kind of weather. He knew about cold air but the American cold was more intense than that back home in Canada. It would take a while for him to get used to this kind of weather. He had obtained a scholarship on the study of athletics administration. He was to commence his classes on the eighteenth of January and he was two weeks out. It was said that the school gave two to three weeks leeway to the students so that they would have a detoxification and assimilation to the new climates especially if they were international students. That was music to his ears and also to the ears of the other foreign students and to those non students who have travelled to different countries.

It was torture to one's body. Some time zones were just horrible. It was like having to go to Alaska where during a certain time of the year, it is either always dark or always light. When the human body that is not accustomed to such an environment is subjected to climate changes outside their zone of comfort, it can be sheer torture. Torrance slept for two straight days. He just lay on his bed even when he was not sleeping. He just felt too tired to want to get up to do anything. He remembered

Nancy and though he was glad to have known her, he still had some unanswered questions about her past and especially why she had refused to divulge her age. He really loved her and he did not imagine himself loving anyone else. He was still young and could easily become the best in his event as far as athletics was concerned. That however was a path that had already been taken. His focus was not where it should be and partaking in sport was not an option for him. It would take Nancy to bring him back to his top form. A dream that would only come true in his dreams. Torrance woke up and after the usual preparations to look presentable, he made his way to the school cafeteria. He got a few stares here and there from those who remembered him. He acknowledged them and wished that he could be acknowledged in return by love. His thoughts about Nancy became chronic to the extent that he soon found himself drinking once again.

3 HIGHLY SENSITIVES.

Torrance did not know that as a highly sensitive person, stress would deplete his iron levels and in turn the body of such a person with this trait would become lethargic or crave whatever it felt would restore the depleted reserves. Torrance had tasted wine and beer, the two most concentrated iron rich sources of this nutrient. His mind led him to action. He bought a bottle of wine from the nearest liquor store and indulged. He drunk himself to a stupor. At times, he would just pass out only to find himself sprawled on his bedroom floor and sometimes in the nude. "I am not a drunk" he would tell himself. I just like the taste of wine."

To a teetotaler, this might seem like the epitome of denial even if what Torrance was saying was one hundred percent accurate. If only Torrance knew his genetic makeup much better, he would take appropriate steps to contain his quench for what healed him but also what could destroy him if left unchecked. People like him were like the eagle who grew up thinking that it was a chicken. The storyline goes to say that on a beautiful Sunny day, mother eagle was out foraging for food for her Eaglets.

By some unfortunate turn of events, one of the eggs got pushed out of the nest by an egg predator or by a gust of wind. The egg rolled down the high cliff and miracle of miracles, it landed on a soft patch of vegetation and subsequently rolled itself by a chicken's nest that also had eggs. Mother hen may have questioned her sanity as regards the egg but her maternal instincts only whispered one thing to her. Care for the egg. As nature took its course, all the eggs hatched and five chicks emerged. They were the cutest bunch you would ever imagine and mother hen was proud to be a mommy.

The brood played with each other and as time went by, the chicks began to question the behavior of their brother "Brutus" He was polite, calm and very friendly but he seemed to have a bigger appetite than everyone else. His wings seemed to be larger than those of his siblings and when the played jump, Brutus seemed to outjump and outlast everyone else. It was even rumored in some circles among the dogs and the cats and even the sheep and cattle on this farm where the animals and poultry lived that they had seen him flying and trying to eat the mice only to apologize for his "weird" behavior to them later. This went on and on and it became even scarier when they compared their growth levels.

Brutus was three times as big as the biggest among them who was dwarfed in comparison. It took a brave soul among the other chickens to play with Brutus. The last time he played wrestling, the other sibling broke his leg and that night, the farmer and his family put the poor bird out of its misery and into their stomachs.

Torrance still had the "eagle that thinks it's a chicken" mentality. Not to say that other people were not unique. It was just that Torrance possessed a higher ability on each of the five senses that all human beings possess.

"May I please have a seat? All the other loner spots are taken". Torrance looked up from his table and there was standing in front of him a beautiful lady that he later came to know was a Japanese. "Please sit down. There is more than enough room on this table" said Torrance. She liked to eat alone and was an international student like Torrance. She told Torrance that she at times observed him but only as a by the way kind of notice. She knew he always liked his privacy and sits down with no more than three persons at any given time. "So what brings you here to this school?" After

Funding out that her name was Cassia, he proceeded to meet with her and they ended up being study buddies. Cassia was very talented and intelligent on top of being very empathic, qualities and feelings that drew Torrance ever so close to her.

"Torrance, should you be drinking like that all the time. You have been sipping on your suds more frequently. Do you simply like the taste or do you have a drinking problem?" Cassia had never seen Torrance drunk but rumors had begun circulating that he would buy some liquor and go to his bedroom where he would eat some steak and then drink himself to a stupor and passed out frequently. "No Cassia, I am not an alcoholic.

Sometimes I just like to sip a little bit here and there". I do so mostly in my room because people have the tendency to erroneously judge those whom they see drinking. They may even label you if you read the ingredients on the side sticker if the bottle".

She was not convinced of what her said and with cautious reluctance, respectfully accepted his explanation. Poor Torrance had not the foggiest idea that people like him were one in a million. Why this was so in the genetic pool that was humanity and why it landed on him he could not explain. He did not even know. In class he would write down what was a book in the making when asked to write a one thousand word paper. His ability to concentrate was astounding. His attention to detail was even more perplexing. He would notice things in others that others did not even notice in themselves. His hearing was phenomenal.

Not to say that he was some kind of superhuman. No. It was just that he had a trait dubbed sensory processing sensitivity that was a shared trait by a fifth of the Earth's population at any given time. The tragedy was that many people were completely unaware of this. It is like the eagle raised as a chicken. Its siblings were also birds but may have had fewer strengths than their brother who they thought was kind of weird.

"What are you doing this afternoon Cassia?" asked Torrance. Cassia had nothing to do but a lady does not immediately say nothing. "I will have to check my schedule but am pretty sure my schedule is not too closed ". She replied. "I found this fancy restaurant on the north side of town and wanted to take you there ". Would you do me the honors Cassia? Cassia agreed. Torrance agreed to come pick her up at seven that evening.

Torrance had gotten himself ready an hour early. He was not leaving anything to chance. This was a very ritzy, exclusive and hard to come by restaurant. He had never had of it and a colleague of his in the track team had mentioned it as they practiced and romanced together. Torrance liked what he heard. They served five course meals and he for one had never experienced such meals that were often a preserve for and of the rich.

With a beautiful woman like Cassia on his side, he was going to kill two birds with one stone that evening. It was a Friday evening and students were lounging in the lobby of the women's dormitory. There were other equally well dressed guys and gals who had plans of their own and so no one turned heads by being dressed up. They just all seemed happy to be going out with their best friends.

The television was on and the local stations were airing reruns of law and order. It was an all-day showing and some students were having a blast from the past with a few cups of soda pop that mysteriously seemed to get refilled whenever the thirsty party reached out for a penny they just seemed to drop under the table. Of course everyone knew what was really happening. They did not care and it did not matter to them as long as boundaries and noise barriers were respected.

Thirty minutes remained before the allotted meeting time, Torrance was enjoying the reruns and he even asked the soda pop drinker if he may have some "soda pop". The request was gladly obliged and Torrance relaxed a little bit. He did like the taste of it but was not going to go crazy when he knew that there was a beautiful girl upstairs making herself even prettier for the evening and by extension to him. The lobby was a step down lobby and so the steps leading to the first floor gave a regal ambience to the place.

The dormitory had three floors and Cassia's was the second. Five minutes past seven, a lady in an absolutely stunning sequined dress came down the red velvet steps that led to the main lobby. She turned heads. Even sobered up a few. She was undoubtedly the best dressed woman that Torrance had laid his eyes on since........

"Nancy you look fabulous ". Nancy looked ravishing and gorgeous in the red dress that she had put on to go with Torrance to the Athletes ' opening night gala that was held once a year to honor up and coming athletes from across the nation. Nancy had made it to third place among the finalists and considering the magnitude of the reason it was being held, anyone who was even considered among the top ten was as good as number one.

"Thank you Torrance. You do not look so bad yourself "she replied. Torrance did look stunning himself. He was lanky, tall and well cut. It was as though he was personally chiseled for perfection. The two of them would have easily won trophies for being the best dressed couple in the room.

Torrance got up, every bit the gentleman and acknowledged Cassia. That was the least he could do. Nancy was still in his mind but he knew that there was a difference between a memory and a reality.

The reality was about to accompany him on a date this evening. Torrance had gotten his car detailed earlier that day. He had never been on such a special date with anyone since Nancy and because he did not want anything to go wrong, he took precautions to keep it that way. "I parked the car much closer so that the wind will not play havoc on your hair. I remembered you told me that the wind down here in these parts was not like the winds elsewhere".

Cassia would have kissed him that moment. He took her hand and they walked out of the massive lobby that actually resembled a five star hotel's foyer instead of a University dormitory. They walked out of the tall oak doors and only walked a few steps towards the parking lot. When Torrance said he had moved the car closer, he was actually euphemizing illegally parking on the grass. He had told campus security that it was for a pressing emergency that had to have immediate and close mobility.

They were skeptical but they gave him one hour. There really was no cause for concern since the small space the car occupied had no significant impact on the school transportation network. Torrance opened the door for Cassia and she gladly and elegantly slipped inside. He got into the driver's seat and turned on the Ignition and away they went. Torrance slid in a tape of his friend's favorite artist. It was a good song that Cassia liked. It was a romantically captivating song and its lyrics left the listener in no doubt about what message was being sent to the recipient. I want you.

Cassia noticed that detail. However she did not think that Torrance had any ulterior motives. He was too much of a gentleman for such moves. At least not now she reckoned. Torrance drove very smoothly and carefully as they inched ever so close to their destination. They laughed heartily all the way to the restaurant and Torrance had never seen Cassia looking so very beautiful a million times more than she did tonight. She was simply amazing.

They pulled up to a single level building and a valet met them right at the entrance where he took their vehicle and then left them to walk a blue carpet that was about ten feet from the entrance.

The message that was sent to the patrons who came here was very simple. You are important and not like everyone else. It is the ambience that one felt as they walked towards the restaurant. They were met by the maitre'd who confirmed their reservation and led them towards a booth specifically prepared to cater to the two of them. Torrance wanted to but did not have to pull out the chair for his woman this time. There were people paid to do that. For the price anyone paid to dine here, the least that the establishment could do was have someone to pull out your chair for you. They were assigned their own personal waitress who asked them what they wanted to drink and what appetizers they would like. They both chose the Escargots a LA bourguignonne or snails in butter as well as cream of watercress soup. They were doing a French theme on the appetizers. They thanked the waitress who took both menus and politely reciprocated the thanks. There was no hurry. It was going to be an unjoyful evening.

"Torrance, this place is great. What other surprises do you have in store for me? I just love your kind of surprises" Cassia exclaimed in between mouthfuls. Torrance was equally surprised and elated at the way the evening was going. He was not even thinking about the courses that their waitress was serving them. However, there was no ignoring the main course. France is usually considered as the home of French cuisine so much so that even the word itself is French. French food is served with flair and passion and the French are known the world over for their incomparable food. That reputation was reinforced by the meals they chose. Cassie opted for the cassoulet which was a dish served in a bowl that was made up of braised duck mixed with sautéed onions and marinated beef with potatoes slow cooked in an oven for three hours and then put in a casserole dish. It looked like a pie but upon taking one bite, the palette was simply lost literally in culinary translation.

The taste just exploded in one's mouth as evident in the look on Cassia's face. She ate each spoonful slowly and savored each second. For a brief moment, Torrance was invisible. He was a backbencher and he seemed to understand his invisibility when he took the first bite of his ordered meal. His was the Coq Au vin (coke o vow). Basically it is a traditional French dish of chicken in red wine. It is pieces of chicken that have been marinated and then braised in the oven in red wine and cognac sauce. The whole dish is then garnished in onion and bacon.

Soon, it was time for dessert. They were both at this time too full but managed to have a simple serving of strawberry cheesecake. Then after a cup of decaffeinated coffee, they say down for a while to let the food digest and Torrance reinforced the point that he was appreciative of Cassia and that he was glad that she had come into his life. "Torrance I enjoyed this meal .I was glad that it was with you that we had this meal". Torrance looked at Cassie and reciprocated in kind by telling her that she had changed his perception of friendship and that she was a strong positive influence on him.

A group of so well adorned violin players trooped into the dining hall and started playing serenading music yet no visible recipients were there. Cassia thought that it was just part of the ensemble. That was until they moved closer to the table they were seated at. Then Torrance took a little case from inside his right front pocket of the blazer he had on and proceeded to go on one knee while next to Cassia.

"Nancy, will you marry me? ". Nancy looked at her best friend not quite sure of what she had just heard. "Yes

Torrance. Oh yes". Torrance at that particular moment was the happiest man alive. "Torrance, I had started thinking that you are horrible in taking cues from a person who has been waiting for what seems like centuries for the person to figure out the subtle messages that are being sent". Nancy loved Torrance from the bottom of her heart. She looked at the ring on her finger and it was at that moment that she knew that this was real and that Torrance wanted her to be with him for the rest of their lives. Nancy had been with boys before but it was in high school where no one really wanted to have a boyfriend or girlfriend but just did it anyway because of either peer pressure or they were experimenting.

Nancy's experiments went belly up. She just seemed to be attracting the wrong kind of people. They would start out well and then suddenly they became hideous monsters overnight. With Torrance, she saw a real gentleman. At first as with the guys in her past, she aired to the side of caution looking for any potential bad vibes but got nothing none from Torrance. Eventually she began to open up to him as she did not see anything that might have freaked her out. "So what now Torrance?" Nancy and Torrance looked like two high school teenagers who had no idea what to do. "I guess it is first things first.

We inform our parents and then we look around for a venue, shop around for your wedding dress and then set a date and proceed from there. Nancy hugged her soon to be husband and the two walked hand in hand out of the five star restaurant that Torrance had selected to take Nancy out on a date. The setting had been perfect. It was summer time and Torrance had reserved a table for two at the Hilton hotel's famous brunette and restaurant that was located in the twenty first floor of the hotel. The restaurant had an open too that allowed just enough sunlight to make the guests feel as though they were still on the ground floor in case any had claustrophobic tendencies or phobias that might have otherwise been a problem.

Three days later, Nancy was killed in a grizzly car accident and there was not one but two victims that day who had started their life journey together. Torrance wished that he had been the one who was in the car because as it was, he was a dead man walking. To be without her was like being empty inside. He was angry at life for giving him the best he could ever want and then taking the best away from him.

"Yes, oh Yes Torrance, I will marry you". Torrance felt a feeling of euphoria overtake him. He was the happiest man alive and he could not help but punch himself much to the amusement of the other patrons.   Cassie stood up and Torrance have her the biggest hug possible that she had to nudge him off.

The other patrons all clapped in happiness and later that evening, Torrance and his future wife got two complimentary all bills paid invitations anytime during the next month back to the hotel as they had doubled the reservations with their confirmation of love.

"So Torrance, I guess we need to make this public starting with our parents. "I guess we should Nancy. I guess we should". Cassia was the first to inform her parents who were overjoyed at the news. They liked Torrance very well and had no serious reservations about the choice their daughter had made. Torrance was not a perfect person but he tried to make the most out of every situation for the better. They could not have asked for a better choice of son in law. It was like sweet music listening to his soon to be wife talking about the wedding. She spoke accordingly of the dress that she would like to wear at her wedding and where she would like the ceremony to take place. Torrance was just glad that she had said yes and he was going to m and her the happiest woman on the planet. She was also going to make him the happiest man on the planet.

"Torrance we have to talk about your drinking. Not that you are an alcoholic but it is an issue that we have to address baby".

It was one of the dark subjects that Torrance did not like discussing but that had to be discussed anyway. Torrance was not really an alcoholic. He just had an iron deficiency and Cassia had come across an interesting topic on a certain group of people called highly sensitive people. Such people made up one fifth of the earth population as far as their genetic makeup is concerned. Such people are not by any stretch of the imagination superior to anyone. They just have a different genetic makeup. With some of them, they have an iron deficiency in their systems that can be replenished by eating iron rich foods or drinks. Unbeknownst to many such people, they find themselves craving wine, beer, they love meat as well as liver. When viewed from the outside, they are alcoholics. That is the strange and dad fact that this people have to go through.

Another sad factor about this trait is that energy reserves can be depleted. Cassie also discovered that the trait becomes more of a burden than a blessing when the host does not balance the pros and cons of it. Such people seem to almost have a sixth sense. They are extremely creative and detail oriented. They also tend to be much conserved because of their sensitivity. Since the world around them is generally full of people who are not as sensitive, they have an extremely difficult time relating to the masses. They try and try again but eventually it's back to the drawing board for them. They are kind hearted and always giving of themselves.

They do not like to see anyone in pain and they are pacifists in nature. That is the reason that they are at times falsely mislabeled as anti-social or introverted. That however is far from the truth. They do love people. It is the people that do not seem to love them back. A painful existence emotionally from them.

Especially is it worse for the men because around the globe, men are supposed to be macho and not sensitive. In all fairness, men should have some degree of sensitivity but with highly sensitive men, the degree of sensitivity is higher. If they try to be or act more macho, it backfires and comes out as mediocre. Cassie had done some background on Torrance and found out about Nancy. She would only imagine what he had gone through. It must have destroyed him inside.

She knew this about five months ago because she had noticed that he was not like the other guys. With the gifts that he had, he as a man would naturally be walking around thumping his chest and glorifying himself but the opposite was the truth. He was as docile as a well fed barn mouse. If anything, he shunned the limelight and kept more to himself

"Torrance, could we talk. I have been researching on a very sensitive topic and I felt that the information would be of great benefit to you and to your future endeavors.

It might even explain some issues that you may have puzzled about for a while." Sometimes Torrance wondered if he was the one wearing skirts in the relationship.

He knew that women liked surprises and that a surprise was not a surprise if you were told about it but this just took the cake.

He could not think of anything that he may have perhaps done wrong in their fledgling relationship. If anything, he had just asked the woman to be his missing rib and so he could not fathom what surprise she had in store for him.

His eyes never wandered and so he crossed out that option and he was not violent to her either verbally or physically. He knew that her parents loved him and so he was left in some kind of quandary here. Oh well, he reckoned, it is what it is. It was typical of him given that he did not know what or who he really was, to harbor such fears. He actually was in effect proving his future wife right on her findings. Most men who knew they had nothing to worry about went on about their business waiting to be told or waiting to hear what their wives had to say. They would go about their business like it was of no major concern but Torrance and persons like him were not genetically structured the same way.

To them it was the drums rolling. Someone was about to mention the losers or winners and until then, the suspense was there. A good night's sleep may temporarily alleviate their anxiety but until the paper announcing the results was unfolded, people like him were a bunch of nerves. The iron in their systems could get depleted and Cassie knew this. Torrance's mind thought about wine and a bottle of beer. It was amazing how he could switch from zero to one hundred in a second.

From not thinking about alcohol in any of it forms to taking his jacket and going to his favorite watering hole even when he did not have any money because he knew that Ashley his favorite bartender owed him a favor and it was time to collect. Many people with brothers, sisters, nephews or nieces, fathers, mothers, uncles or whoever else was in the same gene pool, are quick to slap a label on persons or like Torrance. Drunks. They may even call for interventions because to them, and it is in loving innocence, their beloved one is an alcoholic and that is further from the truth.

It is funny that with all the technology available, Medical personnel have not been able to explain this phenomenon. You could have a person who detests alcohol and does everything to shun it suddenly as if on cue, goes on a drinking spree and when they sober up or come to some semblance of normalcy, regret what they did and get consumed by guilt. Alcoholics on the other hand are different. They get consumed by the fact that the bar closed earlier even if it closed at the same time as it did the previous day.

He knew that the night could end badly. He did not know how but he knew it could. He mentally tried to tell his legs to go the opposite direction but it was too late. His nostrils caught one waft of the revelry and the smell of liquor from the pub and the drop of blood was drawn. He was the shark. Anyone who knows shark behavior was welcome to complete this scenario. He became frenzied. He became like a volcano that would not hold back any longer until the last cinder of molten lava was expelled. He sat on his favorite seat and Ashley did not even have to ask what he wanted. He took to the shot of vodka like a duck takes to water. He even did not say hi to his favorite bartender. She wondered what was different with him. Torrance even wondered what was different with him. He took three more shots before he felt calm. He felt normal. His iron reserves had not yet been replenished. He needed a different vintage. He ordered one bottle of Guinness. The concentration of iron within was a roadblock to insanity. He actually calmed down and decided it was enough. He had to go back to the dormitory.

Cassie met Torrance bright and early the next morning at the school cafeteria. It was to her the best venue to explain to him what was in her mind. She knew that the way to a man's heart was through his stomach even if he was going to prepare his own plate. It was Friday and on such a day, the students were more upbeat and looking forward to the weekend and so Torrance being one of them was likewise in a good frame of mind to be more attentive.

"Torrance my dear, you look good love. I need to discuss something with you". Torrance was eager to hear what was in his bride to be's heart as she had seemed anxious. Torrance and Cassie sat down at the corner of the cafeteria or at least one of the corners. "Torrance, you know how I appreciate everything that you have stood for. You are kind, patient polite and loving towards me and you manifest the same disposition towards other people as well". Torrance took a bite out of the sausage biscuit he had served himself. Sausage was one of his favorite foods. It was not by chance that meat was among the favorites of his cuisine meals. "Torrance, when in your life did you take your first drink?"

Nancy was looking pretty in her blue floral outfit that made her look so feminine. She and Torrance were going to spend the afternoon together. They both loved each other and Torrance had arranged the whole excursion. Nancy was fragile and beautiful and each time Torrance saw her, it was like getting the feeling you get when you open a gift. He wanted to constantly maintain that exuberance. They got into the car and drove to the expansive park that was complimented with a beautiful miniature lake with a fountain in the middle. It was quite the most beautiful sight to behold. Torrance and Nancy were deeply in love but they were both old fashioned. They kept boundaries and never displayed any extreme public displays of affection.

They walked over to a clearing a few meters from the edge of the lake, spread the polka dot cloth they had and proceeded to take out the food and drink that they had brought. Nancy was not the one driving and so had packed a bottle of wine to go with the pate that she had prepared.

Torrance saw the sparkling red drink as it seemed to tease him. He had never tasted wine before and he asked Nancy if he could savor a taste. "Torrance, I would not encourage you to but you are old enough. Just sip it and do not gulp it". Torrance nodded his head and took his glass and filled it halfway before first smelling it and then swirled it like he had seen Nancy do like she was an expert sommelier. His taste buds at first rejected the taste but Nancy had told him what to expect. She had told him it takes two to three different sips the first time. By the fourth sip, Torrance thought that the wine was the sweetest drink he had ever tried. Torrance from that day on bought a bottle of wine twice a week. He never knew that he had started down a path that many start and going back would be a battle that takes the effort of every fiber of one's being.

Torrance remembered that scene with Nancy by the lake at the park many years ago. When he thought about it, that initial sip had avalanched to two packs of beer, twelve in each, three times a week. He always tried to conceal this habit because he knew he was drinking more than necessary but to him, he thought it was okay. "Cassia, it was about three, maybe three and a half years ago since I first indulged in drink".

Why do you ask? Have I done something that offended you?" Cassie shook her head and said

"Torrance, you have done nothing wrong to me dear. We are going to get married and before we actually do, I think we can agree that we both have to discuss issues pertinent to our union".

Torrance wondered if he was drinking way too much, not realizing how much he was drinking and Cassie had noticed. "Torrance, you are different from other people ""Oh sweetie...I appreciate......... "She stopped him in mid-sentence. Am not talking about your qualities dear". I am talking about a trait that you have".

Cassie was taking healthcare as her major and Torrance was wondering if she had stumbled upon an issue that affected humans and was excited about it and wanted to share it with him. "Torrance, your drinking is controlling you". Torrance paused and put down the cup of Orange juice that he held in his hand. "How do you mean Cassia?" Torrance, do you like meat? Do you like spinach? She knew the answers to these questions. "Yes Cassia, I do. I may not have the healthiest diet but I try".

Cassie had used a hook to get his attention. Torrance was very strict about criticism and so for Cassia to say this to him albeit in a loving way, it stung him. Cassia loved her future husband to be and just wanted what was best for them. It was more painful to her that people like Torrance went about their daily lives finding themselves drinking and onlookers label them as drunks. "Torrance, you are what is called a highly sensitive person. Persons like you are special. It is sad that your kind of people are not aware of the special gifts that they have. You have been raised thinking that you are too sensitive, are not crazy about being in crowds and hate noise". You also are very loving. Concepts like jealousy almost never exist within persons like you". Torrance was keenly listening. She was either a very good guesser or she took her research seriously.

He however wondered where the alcohol came in. "The look on your face is telling me that you are asking where the alcohol comes in and also why the spinach was mentioned." Torrance's queries were getting warmed up.

"Cassia, I am listening" Cassia continued" Torrance, most highly sensitive people lack or have a serious deficiency of iron. Usually, as they grow older, they seem to get tired easily and in some cases, those with poor diets tire out easily even more than those with a good diet"

Torrance was watching the news in his living room watching the television and the news just never seemed to change. Violence, corruption and lack of empathy in humanity. Today was the tenth anniversary of his marriage to Cassia. He took a shower, shaved his face and put on his best suit. Today was a very special day for him.

Cassia looked very beautiful. Her beauty was superlative. They had always looked like the perfect couple from the time they met and he was thankful he did. He put on his shoes and prepared for the day.

He was going to meet her where they usually met each year for the last seven years. It was always a special moment at this time every year.

Then he saw her. He remembered the day they met. The most beautiful girl

He pulled up with the flowers that he had in his hand and they were freshly picked as he had instructed his florist. Cassie deserved only the best.

"Torrance, you drink not because you like drinking. You always feel guilty whenever you drink and that is because you feel bad but cannot stop it. You have a special trait that in the scientific world is called sensory processing sensitivity". You told me that you find yourself moving from job to job for reasons you cannot explain. That is a characteristic of most people like you. You are so detail oriented so much so that in any workplace, you understand the details of the job faster, better and more proficiently than the average person and when you feel it is not challenging, you unlike other people will not go to work for the sake of going. You need either to be given something more challenging or you quit". People like you become scientists, Doctors, heads of corporations and the crème de la crème of society because of your trait.

It becomes more enhanced when you know that you have it". Torrance did not honestly know what to say. What does someone say in a situation like this? One is just told that they are not who they are and that they have been like an eagle raised up as a chicken. "So Cassia, about the alcohol. You are saying that I find myself drinking a lot to replenish my iron reserves? Cassia nodded. Torrance was dumbfounded. It gave him a sense of astonishment and relief at the same time knowing the information he had just imbibed.

Torrance   and the best men arrived at the venue that he and Cassia had set aside for the wedding. It was an old baroque building that was a traditional French styled theme structure. It was a three story building that was built at the turn of the century. It has served many purposes during its tenure. It has been a school, it had been a museum and it had been an art gallery. Many living couples had wed here and today it was Cassia and Torrance.

The groom and his entourage of men had arrived earlier that day and made sure that everything was going to be perfect. That was four hours ago. It was now twelve thirty in the afternoon and Torrance had made sure that he was not going to keep Cassia waiting. She deserved nothing but the best. He was so excited he could not wait to put the ring on her finger and subsequently on her heart for the rest of their natural lives. Cassia walked inside the hall at exactly one minute past one. She had the most beautiful and modest yet modern wedding dress that the gathered had ever seen. She wore a sequined satin dress and a veiled head cover. Torrance smiled as his bride's father walked her down the carpeted aisle while the assembly of people craned their heads to catch a glimpse of this beautiful girl.

Torrance walked over to where Cassia was. It had been seven years since they had been married. She had made him into a real man and removed the veil of falsehood that life had made him think he was. She had removed this veil to reveal the person that he was actually meant to be and as time went by, he became stronger and stronger. She had given him a daughter whom he adored dearly.

On this day, he decided that her grandmother would be best suited to baby sit Gracie their daughter, as Cassia and him had their time together. "Meeting you was the best thing that ever happened in my life Cassia. You gave me a second chance in life. That and a wonderful daughter who looks like a carbon copy of you.

I simply adore you and love you so much. Cassia remained quiet. "Cassia, forgive me for all the horrible things that I did to you that may have upset you my dear beloved. Thank you for giving me a second chance in life my dear." Cassia remained quiet. Torrance had started a non for profit organization to bring awareness to people about the under advertised or mentioned trait that many people had yet never knew anything about. He had also started writing books on the subject.   That was another credit that he owed Cassia.

She had made him believe in himself so much so that she encouraged him to bring out his strength of being detail oriented.

His attention to detail had enabled him to start writing books, something he never believed he could have ever done in his life. He even had a book titled after this girl that he had married many years ago. He looked at her and thought that she was by now bored to death about his babbling. So he took the flowers that he had bought and gave them to her. He then hugged her and spoke to her further for a few more minutes. Thanks to

Cassia, Torrance had started a revolution in the world of psychology and a blitz of information that made a small yet substantial debt in the arena of ignorance that had started a domino effect that had helped so many persons.

He even named the foundation the Cassia foundation for highly sensitive people. It sometimes made him wonder how he was so fortunate to have been in the lives of two beautiful yet talented women. If there were any other men like him, they were the happiest men around. Nancy and Cassia changed Torrance like no one has done before and Torrance really hoped that he may have made this two wonderful girls better persons as they had done him. He remembered the laughs and cries that they had together, the joys and sorrows that they all shared. Memories of them made him sigh lovingly.

They really had fun together. Torrance turned around and proceeded to leave after having spent some time with Cassia. "Cassia, you know what, we do not have to spend another year doing this. We can do this more often. He laid the bouquet of Red roses by her tombstone and turned around to walk back to his car.

Torrance reflected on his life. Two beautiful women had come and gone. He was left with a younger and smaller version of one of them and he looked upwards towards the sky with a pious look. Torrance had travelled half way around the world away from his home only to be told by a woman he loved that in effect, his life had been one big lie. He had lived until he met the woman whom he had just memorialized tell him who and what he really was. He had died to his old self and become a new better person thanks to the woman who lay buried eighty meters away from him. Yvonne, Nancy and Cassia. I need to write a book on these people. His life redefined and gave new meaning to a former now deceased Prime Minister's statement. Torrance's truths about himself had just sat on a chair and began tying their laces. It would be a while before he caught up with the truth.

"A lie has travelled halfway around the world while the truth is still tying its shoes"...

Sir Winston Churchill (British Prime Minister)

KENROY

4 A MAN OF THE BOYS

The Stockholm syndrome derives its name from a bank robbery that occurred years ago in Stockholm Sweden but which definition and example traverses geographical boundaries. It may as well be called the Johannesburg or Madrid or Nairobi or Oklahoma City or Washington or Paris or whatever town the robbery may have happened Syndrome.

It was when the robbers held the unfortunate customers hostage in the hopes of getting some kind of ransom that some of the customers developed a sick kind of bond with the robbers in the hopes of perhaps getting the robbers to soften their mistreatment, if any.

At first, this may seem like a brilliant idea and it has indeed worked in some cases. Cooperation with your abductors, captors or with those with the means to harm you is a way of bringing hope of survival to what may otherwise end up as a potential catastrophe. Sometimes however, things take a turn for reverse when the abducted become one with the abductor. When this gradual change happens, an imprint has taken place so much so that the threat becomes the savior. It happens even during abductions.

Missing persons who may have been kidnapped become so used to the abductor to the twisted point where the abductor will even leave for a week or two and come back and find a steak and beer waiting for him or her. Such are the mysteries of life.

"The seventeen year old shut the drive through window and prevented the rude customer from yelling and shouting any more vitriol and choice words. The customer seemed inebriated and incoherent. Upon further and closer scrutiny, it was clearly evident that the same profanity using customer may have been seeing hallucinations because he was not able to reach out to the steering wheel. He was reaching out to a somewhat fictitious steering wheel a foot away and thus the reason the window was shut and the police on speed dial. There

Was a big difference listening to legitimate concerns and like listening to nonsense?

It was another day at the glamorous restaurant where the barely legal teenager worked. At seventeen, he was twice as mature as the other employees who were twice as old as him. He was arguably the best worker in this fancy restaurant and even though the green eyed monster may have appeared in some of the employees regarding his work ethic and elevated work standards, facts were facts.

He was the best employee. He did not even have to strut around thumping his chest like most persons who felt that they were the best. He had come aboard at sixteen and was green behind the ears. In one year he had become a natural leader in this organization. He had seen employees come and go. He had seen others come in the morning and leave two hours later at break time.

The nurse came into the waiting room and gave the good news to the relatives of Jane and Paul Jennings. It was a healthy bouncing baby who by all vital statistics was the prime example of health. The two parents were in their mid-twenties and this was their second child. The first was a girl. She was now a three year old. The age gap was by all means healthy as the two kids were. Ariel the first borne was the prettiest thing that one could imagine.

No doubt the two children were a blessing to the two parents.

In seventeen years the young man and his sister had been the epitome of good children. They were by no means perfect. They had made mistakes like most normal kids make.

They were excellent at school and had grades that could open doors to any college. They however stayed humble. They took everything with a pinch of salt. By all necessary means, they should be shouting at the rooftops about their achievements. To the two, they were passionate about what they did. Any rewards reciprocated by society were to them collateral.

At fifteen, Kenroy had skipped two grades already. While his peers were twiddling their thumbs wondering what answers were, he had his ear buds on waiting for the teachers to say "see you Tomorrow and read page xyz as your assignment" Secrets are okay with everyone. In some families however, some secrets are just too deep and painful. The family was going to make sure that the secrets remained that way. Secretive.

Kenroy pulled up the parking lot and parked at his favorite spot with his trademark parking style. The car faced frontwards in stark contrast to the other cars. As long as it was not illegal or double parked, there was really nothing wrong with how he parked

Kenroy greeted the Manager and the other staff members as he usually did and out on his name tag that had been pinned on the notice board. It was the usual day as the others. Nothing out of the ordinary. The board showed who was not going to show up and who would be late and also who was given a good review by customers.

Kenroy put on the drive through headset and proceeded to get his own cash register. It was four in the afternoon and he was scheduled to be there until midnight. He was touted as being the next Manager and they could start training him when he attained the legal age. He knew the ins and outs of the restaurant better than most people and it was because he was passionate about his job. However, Kenroy had other ambitions. He was planning to open his own recording studio one day and he worked here at the glamorous restaurant to get additional funds saved that would help him achieve his endeavors. Given the amount of hours that he was working at the restaurant, it was feasible that he would easily achieve his goals very soon. After he finished high school, Kenroy managed to get a place at a prestigious University in a neighboring town. He was thrilled at the prospect and would not wait to tell his cousins, friends and relatives about what just happened after he had read the acceptance letter from the College.   "Finally, its baby steps towards my recording dream" he thought to himself.

He already envisioned in his mind a huge office skyscraper tower building on the tenth floor and not so much for prestige but rather for the privacy it would accord him to play his trade. Kentucky's sister Ashley was exuberant and excited for her brother. Ashley herself had procured a place at one of the colleges within their hometown that was by no means comparable to Kenroy's in stature but was indeed a kindred academic institution that without easily give the best, as seen in the eyes of society, a run for its money. She was already halfway through her education and told Kenroy that if he wanted any kind of help with his homework, he knew her number. Of course this was meant in the most living and supportive way. Ashley knew that her brother did not need any tutoring especially since he had been known to correct his own instructors while in high school. Memory had two months before commencing his first semester. That was ample time to get organized for four years or more that would either make or break him.

Kenroy loved his stepfather as much as his biological one who had passed away ten years ago due to kidney failure. It was a painful transition but the man he now called dad had made the transition smooth and never hoovered or put his foot down in reaffirming his new position. He lovingly let time, love and patience take its course. Kenroy and Ashley despite initial reservations accepted him into the fold and mostly due to his humble and hands off methods.

"Grandmother, have you heard the news?" His father may have passed away but his grandmother lived on, every bit a reminder to him about her son. "Bits and pieces of it Kenroy. You are here now and so you can tell me in detail". Kenroy gladly repeated the news to her. She could remember such a scene thirty years ago with her now deceased son when he got a letter from the very same school that Kenroy was going to. Deja vu in reality.

"I am so happy for you Kenroy. Your father...first father could be very proud and pleased of the success you accomplished and the family tradition that you carried on" No doubt, if genetics were to get credit, this family had very good ones academically. "Thank you grandmother. It was a struggle getting here and I really hope to achieve my dreams of getting my own recording studio and helping other people achieve their dreams no matter which career they choose ". Kenroy was not mincing his words. He had seen the way people lived in other parts of the world and was very fortunate to have what he had. To him, it was time to pay it forward and this was the way he knew how to.

He had to do some downsizing first. He had to sell his vehicle that was too big and with a very spacious interior and settle for something low key or possibly two door. It would take time but he would get there. He also needed to buy some dormitory furniture because as good and modern as the furniture he had seen the school offered, his taste differed slightly from the school's interior decorator.

He had saved enough to buy some of the equipment that he could use. He was not going to be an artist himself but he was going to show budding and upcoming entrepreneurs how they would bring out their talents and skills much better. He had even reserved and requested a one bedroom for himself and had agreed to spend extra money for the additional space and privacy that came with it.

That is when Kenroy began to find out that sometimes, what glitters is not necessarily gold. Out of nowhere as if coming from the woodwork, some of the relatives started the most malicious rumors one could imagine. Kenroy even began to question the reality of his past association with some of this people. The things they were saying and the timing were suspect. His own mother's sister had begun to question the authenticity of the origins of Kenroy. In other words, she alleged that Kenroy's mother was hiding a deep dark secret that she did not want anyone to know and it was only after having a bitter dispute with her younger sister that she threatened to spill the beans on the charade that she called Kenroy's family.

Given the nature of the allegations, it was understandable to see why Kenroy had stopped referring to his mother's sister as Aunt and this was the only time that he referred to her mockingly as Cecilia my mother's younger sister. Ashley had taken a completely different and more extreme approach. She completely disowned her Aunty, blocked her and wanted nothing to do with her.

Their Aunt had claimed that the death of their father was no accident and that the whole entire died-of -kidney failure and that it was years of meticulous planning that gradually made their father's health deteriorate to the point of death. The aunt father claimed that the toxic poison that was used when administered in small amounts was undetectable yet potentially dangerous to the internal organs of the victim. The Aunty had gone so far as to even question the time frame of the demise. Such a poison when administered in small undetectable amounts takes on average two years to slowly yet painlessly devour the key organs of the body. Kenroy thought that the timing of such allegations was horrible.

He had just received good news and his mother and step father had come a long way in their relationship to the point of his stepfather being completely welcomed despite years of reservation from other family members. Ashley was close to their biological father and it has especially taken her years to accept him so for her Aunty to say such horrible things was a betrayal. What was worse than the horrible news was the person dispensing the news.

The brother and sister met at one of the local restaurants that evening as they had many unanswered questions to ask. "Hi Ashley. My apologies to you for cutting short your vacation to come back to the city". Ashley hugged her younger brother and said" It was my pleasure especially since our Aunt had started acting the fool". The waitress handed the menus to the two young people and gave them time to decide what they wanted. Ashley ordered a medium to well done steak while Kenroy ordered his favorite. Spaghetti and meatballs.

The two talked about general life styles and then Ashley finally broke the ice "Aunty is acting and behaving very strangely. She had been coming to the house and picking fights with Dad for no apparent reason".

Mom and she almost came to punches the other day when it was just the two of them. I had just arrived from out of town and had just unpacked when she came knocking at the front door yelling "Annabelle Harriet Jennings, you need to come out here. We need to talk ". Mom came down and opened the door. Aunty seemed so riled up and her speech was somehow incoherent. She was accusing mom of stuff but I could not hear exactly what was being said because mom shut the front door as if protecting my prying ears from hearing damaging information.

"Ashley, whatever is going on is something serious. Mom's sister is not one to make wild accusations unless she is really on to something. Remember eight years ago when she claimed that the nice plumber who fixed the leaking faucet was purposely sabotaging the pipes in the boiler room to make them leak so he could be called out here again and get paid for his own damage? "We all thought her insane or overly imaginative. It turned out that the plumber was doing the same thing to other clients and then reaping the rewards until someone called him out one day". As it turned out, Kinray remembered the incidents. Apologies at the time were in order for their Aunt. "Kenroy, is it possible that we do not see or know the whole entire picture of what is really going on? As painful as some things may be, why don't we give aunty a chance to explain herself to us since mom and dad have slapped her with a restraining order"? We are adults and therefore cannot be stopped from visiting our own aunty. She has not shown any violent streaks and so there is nothing to worry about with her"

5   A TWIST IN THE TALE

Kenroy listened to his sister. She always spoke sensibly. He saw no harm in taking this course of action. Furthermore, what harm was there in asking about matters relating to their late biological father. He was indeed their father and not just some stranger who elicited some kind of leftover attention. So it was decided that they would politely approach their aunty at a convenient time.

Ashley lived fifty miles away at the town where her campus was located and came home twice a week. In all reality, she did not have to stay at school but the thing that was preventing her was the long drive home. It was roughly a little over one hundred miles and that five days a week added up to a lot of mileage, West and tear as well as the use of gas. So it was only prudent that she comes home once a week guaranteed and perhaps two if there was gas and if the car was in good shape.

"Ashley good morning" said Michael to his step daughter. "Good morning dad". Ashley saw in Michael a man who had come in and became a shoulder to cry on when the three of them were in a period of loss and mourning. He had come as a friend of the family gradually and had taken his time while the bereaved took time to mourn.

He took the kids for dinner sometimes and could just sit as mother and two kids reminisced. Eventually they saw no harm coming from him and accepted him. Really he started off as an older brother but graduated to stepdad and eventually be was given the keys to the daddy chair by everyone, a role he played well and full of love for everyone.

It was inconceivable that anyone would hate this man. The common cliché is if it's too good to be true, it's not true. Why people say it is true defies logic. Perhaps different verbiage is in order.

Aunt Sally knocked opened the door in response to the knock that she heard. Her choices were narrowed to three. The mailman, the police or a bill collector. Perhaps two if the last was omitted. She had no bills. "Come in kids" Kenroy and Ashley were ushered into the house where their Aunt lived by herself. She was not the marrying type and was not interested in men. "Strange woman" Kenroy thought to himself. The way she went around peddling what was in his mind lies and half-truths and slander were prime examples as to why she was still single. "This is quite the surprise given that an in everyone's crosshairs at the moment" said their Aunty.

"Actually we are still zooming in" thought Kenroy but kept such a thought to himself. The poor woman had already hang herself way before being in anyone's cross hairs. "We need to talk to you about the door slamming, name calling as well as arguments and accusations that are being flung around wildly and in a very serious and damaging manner"

Their Aunt looked at them. "Tea is almost ready. Please join me for a cup of tea kids "She led them to the verandah outside and went back in to the kitchen and brought out a plate of croissants and warm milk. On the side was some butter and a variety of jelly of choice.

Kenroy backtracked on his earlier negative thoughts on her. He felt she was playing hard to get.   She could easily disarm any man just by such a simple yet exquisite presentation of food. "So Aunty, please let us know what has been going on recently especially between you and your sister. It really bothers us that secrets are being kept er...secretive but the contents of the secrets are spilling out and making quite the scene" Ashley threw the opening salvo and her Aunt Sally simply looked at her and said nothing at first initially.

"Kenroy and Ashley, you know I love your mother very much and any conflicts or disagreements that may arise are simply family related. "Well Aunty, remember that your definition of family changed since we came along and besides, you two are not doing a very good job of keeping family affairs discreet. Even Mr. Tom who lives in the other side of the street had taken to putting his armchair on his front porch in order to make sure he gets the rare glimpse of family affairs gone wild. So technically it is becoming a neighborhood affair". "So what is it really about you and Mother that has gotten you guys almost coming to fists?"

"Kids, I appreciate you guys coming over because of your concern for peace. However, I feel that you need to ask your mother what is really going on. It is something that may turn dangerous if not addressed". The kids look perplexed but they took their Aunt at her word. They could not honestly decipher what was going on. They felt sorry for Michael as he was caught in the middle of all these squabbles. The kids and their Aunt ate the croissants and spent more time with their Aunt, helped her bake a cake that she was going to contribute to the neighborhood security meet the next day.

The kids left their Aunt's house at around five pm and headed to their house. They had discussed enough of the squabbling for one day and decided they would continue tomorrow since it was going to be a Sunday afternoon and Ashley was not expected back at school until the following Monday

"Hi kids, I saw you going to your Aunts place. Is everything okay my dears? "We just went to see how she is doing. We noticed that Aunt Sally has been a bit edgy lately and just wanted to make sure she was okay mom". Michael was in the kitchen and wiped his hands on the towel he had been using to dry his hands. "Are you kids okay?"

The kids nodded and acknowledged Michael while assuaging him that all was alright. He looked at them and nodded as one who was satisfied by what heard but in actuality, he did not believe a thing they said. He had noticed that the two sisters had been feuding verbally and though he kept a respectable distance when it came to family affairs, he was the head of the house and standing by was not in his repertoire of doing things. The kids went to the living room and sat down while Ashley turned the television to the movie channel.

"What do you think is happening Kenroy? I know when we are being taken for a ride. No one wants to say anything and whatever they say or try to say, it is or will probably be half-truths"

"Maybe so Ashley said her younger brother but let us get to hear what has to be said first before we judge anyone" Ashley respected her younger brother. He was indeed more mature than most people twice his age. Michael brought some cookies to the two youngsters and asked them if he could do anything for them. "Actually Michael, there is something you can do for us. Tell us what is really going on with the two women". "Kenroy, I know as much as you guys do. Your mother does not talk very much about divulging the details to me ". With that, Michael turned around and walked back to the kitchen to finish preparing supper. He was a great cook and the kids always enjoyed his cooking.

Michael went over to his wife as she joined her two kids in the living room. He kissed her goodnight and wished the kids the same.

Two minutes of silence passed since he went back upstairs. "We need to get away from here very fast and as soon as possible" The kids were scared. "What is it mother? What is happening? "Their mother was evidently shaken up by something." Michael is not who he is making himself out to be". The kids were initially curious but now they were completely aroused by what they were hearing. "Your father did not die from natural courses kids as has been brought out". Kenroy stood up in utter shock not knowing what he should do or say in reply to what his mother was saying. "So what was the cause of his death?" Their mother was evidently distraught but it was maternal love that kept her strong.

"Ashley, Kenroy, the only real thing about this marriage is the three of us" At this point, even Ashley who was usually the more composed of the two had to ask a pertinent question, the elephant in the room so to speak. "Does Michael have anything to do with this mom? Their mother scribbled down on a paper "act natural kids. If Michael suspects I have told you anything, he will become a maniacal psychopath and become violent". "Mom please change the channel.

Not everyone likes to watch sobby chick flicks" said Kenroy. If Michael had been or was listening, it was not evident. If anything, he was sound asleep by the faint snoring that was just audible. It was one of the times that they had never listened to a more beautiful sound. "Twenty five years ago, I met your father. Him and Francis or Michael as he aliases himself, were business partners. They ran a small bookshop and were by societal standards successful. When I met your Dad, he was hardworking and friendly and both he and Francis loved seeing me at their store"

The kids were speechless. They could not believe what they were hearing but they were nonetheless hearing it. Thoughts zoomed through the children's minds as they listened to their mother. They never saw Michael or Francis or whatever his name was during the first thirteen years of being with their original parents. There was no sighting of him either in any family functions or at their house. He simply was not there. Not in pictures or even any mail. His name, image or mention thereof of his existence was nonexistent. The question in the kid's minds was if their Aunt Sally's actions had anything to do with it. "Kids, I told Aunt Sally about the charade that was going on and her behavior is scripted. It is a ruse so as not to arouse any suspicion in Michael ". We should not all just suddenly change our pattern of doing things otherwise it may raise suspicion"

The kids decided that it was best to go to sleep and continue this conversation at a more convenient time. Ashley asked her mother one last question for the night. "Is he capable of hurting you while we sleep?" Not at all darling. My being alive is the m win reason that he will not hurt me. However, I am always cautious. We can never be too sure if anything. Overconfidence is the biggest weakness that a person can display".

Ashley was not too reassured of this answer that was vague. Kenroy was already thinking of planting a listening device in the room when Michael went to work. That however would be a dead giveaway if it was discovered. Kenroy was the man of the house now because the other one was fictitious. He did not even have proper use of his name and he was a loose cannon morally and physically. Kenroy was going to be half awake this night and for that matter all coming nights even if it meant postponing his college education to protect his mother. It was not going to be easy but it has to be done.

Michael woke up the following Sunday Morning at six. Someone needed to remind him that the entire purpose of the weekend was to relax and forget about the hustles and bustle of weekly working or on whatever day a person's weekend fell on. He beat the eggs and poured them over the hot grease in the pan.

He swirled the eggs around until the eggs started taking the conventional image of fluffiness. He then put the pan on one of the other heating coils that had not yet been used yet. He then took ten oranges and squeezed them into a tall cylindrical container that he intended for everyone to self-serve. He took silver foil and covered the eggs that he placed atop a small shallow pan that had some warm water so as to keep the eggs moist.

After preparing the bacon and made some fresh coffee, he went and turned on the television to be catch up with the latest news. Despite the perception that many may have heard of him, he knew how to put a meal together.

Michael got up and went back to the main bedroom. His wife was still asleep and she looked ever so sweet.

Thirty years ago, this beautiful woman walked into the bookstore he worked in and he could never at the time and even now, take his mind off of her. She was not like the other women. There were others who came to the bookstore or wherever he would find them. This one was different. Her modesty, her humility and her demeanor made the other women at the time and even now pale in comparison. There was however a roadblock to his getting her. The roadblock came in the form of a man called Nicholas. Nicholas in all fair did not know that talking to this woman would create so much strife.

Nancy was her name and they immediately connected the very first time their eyes locked. It may not initially have been love at first sight but it was definitely good chemistry at first bite. She had appeared out of nowhere with a small but substantially big cake that she had cooked for the two newcomers who had come to the town and opened a bookstore that the townsfolk sorely needed. That saved them at least one hundred miles since the other bookstore was fifty miles away at a different county. "Thank you for the cake er....... "Nancy. Nancy Stevens" Nicolas was very grateful and standing next to his copartner Francis, they thanked her for such a nice welcome. "Here you go boys, try a sample" At that particular moment, the phone rang and Francis excused himself".

Nicholas took the bite from Nancy and he momentarily had to take a sit to savor the cake. Nancy was flattered. She was single and quite frankly, Nicholas wondered if there was something wrong with this woman who made any pastry chef look like a novice be single. He was not being judgmental. He was just wondering. "Life sometimes is strange"

Nancy left right before Francis came back to the front register and inquired of the woman" She had to leave Francis" said Nicholas. Francis took one of the saucers that the cake woman as he referred to her had brought for them. That was a very good gesture and also very kind of her to do what she had done. Nicholas agreed. None of them had bothered to take down her number to even thank her a second time. That would have been the prudent thing to do. A little too late.

Michael lay down next to his wife. She was very beautiful and had aged very little from the first time he had seen her three decades ago. It was her attitude about life that made her look so content. In all fairness the healthy meals she cooked without looking like a health fanatic are what endeared her to Nicholas and now to Francis.

Ashley woke up at around eight o'clock and after going through the usual cleansing rituals associated with humans, she went downstairs where she found her already prepared plate of bacon, scrambled eggs and two pieces of toast. The plate was warm, edible and filling. "What was that mom said about Michael?" she thought to herself. This man definitely knew how to put a plate together. Her mother joined her ten minutes later and the two girls sat down at the table, half asleep and munching away. "Mom, did you have a good night sleep?" I did sweetie".

Michael was watching the news in the living room. He loved the news. He always did from the time his wife really got to know him. He loved the news when he worked at the bookstore.

The two women and Kenroy had never met anyone in their life who loved the news as Michael did. He rarely drank anything but when he did, he was a true gentleman.

"Mom, we are still in the dark regarding your situation. What is it that you are trying to tell us that has your sister so riled up even if it is scripted? Script or not, something is going on and now we are involved. So what gives?" "Ashley, Michael is going out of town this afternoon at two. He will not be back until Tuesday ". "We simply cannot wait. This suspense is seriously killing us". Kenroy had just walked in the room and caught the last whisper.

"Nancy, did you tell the kids about my trip later today?" Ashley nodded her head and acknowledged Michael. It was one of those times when she was glad that he was leaving them. "Great breakfast Michael. You always know how to get the family off to a new start". "Anything for my family". Michael they went upstairs to pack his suitcase. It was a business trip "Kids, before I met Francis, you obviously know that I was with your dad. I got to know him very well after I gave him a taste of my cake" Kenroy wondered if that was a metaphor for something he could not respectfully bring himself to ask. "It is not what you think so you can get your head out of the gutter son. I saw your face drop. You can pick it back up"

"I actually took a cake to the bookstore that your dad used to work at and Michael Francis was his copartner"

"It was one neck of a cake or very tasty if it is causing all this strife and unease around here". Nancy told the kids that Francis was so jealous because he did not get to taste the cake by my hands. I gave your dad a small taste and I could have done the same for Francis had he not gone to answer a phone call at the back of the store. Michael Francis I later came to know, became so jealous just because I did not feed him cake"

Kenroy and Ashley were listening and they must have both been glad that their step father was not their first father. If a slice of cake made a grown man pout, it was a good choice that his mother had made by not marrying him years ago.

"So putting the cake aside, what is it about Michael that is freaking you out? Is there more than meets the eye with him?

"Many years ago children, your father decided that he wanted to go back to law school. He was a very intelligent man and after he met me and we fell in love, he wanted to provide more for me and his family that was soon to be you when the time came. I told him that I was very comfortable with what he was doing and if he wanted to go back to school, it was a personal decision he would make and as long as we spent time together, I did not mind whatever he decided to do.

"So how does Michael come into the picture? Ashley was basically speaking for her brother by asking that question. "Michael blackmailed your dad five years after we got married". It came about that your Dad had taken a loan to start the bookstore business and he accidentally misappropriated the amount that was supposed to be given to the Bank. The bank wanted to see his bookkeeping records to see how their money was being spent. Your father honestly did not misappropriate anything. Matter of fact, he caught the mistake that he had made and it was an error he made and wanted to go and tell the Bank about it. However, Michael was Jealous of me and him and threatened to tell the Bank about this discovery. He went back and forth with Michael telling Michael that he would go to the Bank and report the discrepancy. Your father would lose everything he had worked so hard for and so much so that he did not want to jeopardize you kids future and so he kept quiet and gradually died after a losing battle with his health ".Michael then saw his chance and Continued his slanderous blackmailing by telling me to be his wife if I did not want to be homeless '. "Kids, I thought about you guys. I was pregnant and I only wanted what was best for you kids" "Please forgive me ". Ashley and Kenroy could not believe their ears. They were staying in the same house as someone who was basically their by default and blackmail. Someone who they shared their deepest darkest secrets with was living with them and by all token, he seemed to be as innocent as a dove.

Kenroy was taken aback by all this. Michael or whatever his name is had been so good to him. They fixed their car together, spent time together and even cooked food together. A real romance. What was really happening?

His mother could not be lying to him. She had no need to. If his real father had died, why couldn't Michael just do what comes naturally and just fall in love with his mother and live together like other couples who may have lost a loved one in death. There was no need for games. "So how long does he intend to keep up with this charade mom?" Kenroy asked. "As long as we have a roof over our heads dear " came the reply. Kenroy would not reconcile the fact that Michael would be so charming and at the same time so evil in one. Something was not right with this picture.

Their mother begged the kids to act normally so as not to arouse any suspicion from Michael. "Well, that is now easier said than done. We will just keep on pretending as act as we were before. That should not raise a single shred of suspicion".

Their Aunt Sally came by the next day. Michael was gone on business and could not be back for one more day. Sally came to talk to their mother and she never let the kids talk to

Sally since they already knew what they needed to know and that was sufficient. Sally came over still in a riled up state and the kids were wondering why she was still putting up pretenses. Michael was not here and so she did not need to pretend anymore.

She bade the kid's goodbye after talking to their mother for about thirty minutes and then left. She did not seem too happy. She was even more upset leaving than when she had arrived. Such was the life that was around them. Aunt Sally seemed to be more affected by whatever it was that was going on around their extended family.

Michael arrived the next day and came bearing gifts. The kids were amazed at his nerve. He was going around like there was nothing going on. He did not go to work the next day because he wanted to spend time with his wife Nancy and kids that he had not seen for the last two days. There was a knock on the door about three in the afternoon about five hours from the time Michael had arrived and taken a small nap. It was their Aunt Sally who came over.

"Hi Sally. It's good to see you.' said Michael. "It's time we started speaking the truth around here before I go crazy Michael. One day the truth will come out and there will be pain, betrayal and hunger from all sides. We have to get to the bottom of this today ".

The kids were listening keenly and wondering what was going on. Had the two been fighting among themselves? Sally left abruptly but had created enough of a stir to get some tongues wagging. Their mother came downstairs to see what the commotion was all about." Okay, what is going on around here Michael? We really need to know the truth. Why are you really here Michael and why did our Aunt Day something about keeping things real". Said Kenroy. Ashley added her thoughts. "Yes Michael, it's time you came clean. We know who you really are and you might as well come clean. We are fed up of the double standards around here. Why are you really here Michael?"

"Okay, you got me. I will come clean". You are kids many years ago, I met your mother while I worked at the bookstore. It was love at first sight and we knew we wanted each other and to be together forever as man and wife". We got married....

"You got what? When did you get married if it was our dad that had been with mom since we were born? So how is it possible that you say "We got married "? The kids and their mother were listening and they looked at their mother to see her reactions. She was perfectly silent and attentive as though she already knew what was going to be said next.

"Kids, I have to tell you something ". The kids looked at their mother with a puzzled look. What could their mother tell them that would add to this circus that they had been given free front row seats to already? Their mother was the innocent one and what she was about to say was simply a reaffirmation of what they already thought about Michael and to some extent Sally.

"Michael is your real father kids" There was a profound silence for ten while minutes. No one was staring at the ceiling or at any corner of the house. The kids might have been having crazy thoughts about what they wanted to say. How was it that Michael was their father yet they only knew that their real father Nicholas was their true father? It was all so strange.

"Nicholas was a good man. At least there is nothing confusing about that. He was honest, kind and approachable whether at the workplace or at home. Before your mother and him got married, we were married. We just kept it silent ".

The kids were really listening to what was being said. Now. No one was interrupting. "We got you two kids but a tragedy occurred. I came to this country a few years before I met your father and my permit to stay here expired. If I took you kids with me back to my country it would be difficult to raise you there. I did not have the means to give you guys the lifestyle that all kids need and so I was left with one choice".

Nicholas was a good friend to Francis and he was the best man at the wedding of Francis and Nancy. It broke his heart when Francis had to leave. Michael had a big favor to ask of Nicholas and it was quite a big favor. It was not like taking a small loan from someone and repaying later. He was being asked to take care of two living beings. Michael was really like a twin brother to Ni Nicholas. They knew each other before they even knew Nancy. They shared the most intimate secrets and they shared their pains and joys and sorrows together. So he was the only qualified candidate to best raise the two kids.

"So kids, I had to leave for about ten years and Nicholas became so attached to you two that everyone knew, including the two of you, as your father". It broke his heart that I was coming back because he was not ready to give you guys back. Let me be clear that I was not intending to come and "take what was mine". No. I was happy enough knowing that my best friend was the one taking care of you two. I need not ask if he did a good job. You two can speak on that matter".

The emotional landscape of their past was now changing. They began to see their guardians or those that raised them in a whole different light. A day ago they were talking about Michael as though he was a nightmare from a very vile place. They were now seeing him in a completely different light. They also began to see their mother in a different light. Nancy cleared her throat. She needed to speak on the issue. "When Michael left to go back to Trinidad, it was gut wrenching. I had two kids and it was going to be tough on Nicholas. He was like a brother to both Michael and I. He was no stranger to us and as our best friend, he loved you two and he figured that if it was him on the other end of the spectrum, he would have asked the same huge favor from Michael".

As Nicholas grew ever so more attached to his kids, it was difficult for Nicholas to think about losing them to Michael despite the fact that Michael had told him that there was not going to be a disruption of the status quo.

The kids considered Nicholas as their father and tipping those scales especially at the time when the children were not even a decade old could spell disaster emotionally. Nicholas however was not convinced. At the back of his mind, his thoughts betrayed him. He started becoming erratic to the point where his health took a nose dive. He became so sick that he had to take some sick days from work. Michael even decided that it was best of he just disappeared and went somewhere where he could have no communication with either Nicholas or Nancy. It was in the interests of the kids and now of Nicholas.

It was however too late. Nicholas contracted liver cancer and it was too late to reverse it. "Kids, it was very sad watching this man that I came to love take a downward spiral to his death because of the love he had for you guys ". Nicholas was a man in every sense of the word. He loved his kids to the end.

It was then that after a few years that Nancy remarried and Michael came to stay with us. It was even more difficult for him than it was for Nicholas. It was like history repeating itself in deja vu. One may have thought that Michael could come in and presume to be the real father and act as such but he was completely scared and humbled. He felt that he had betrayed and killed his childhood friend. It was very difficult for him to readjust and that is why he kept his distance from you guys.

'Kids , your Aunt Sally felt guilty about the whole arrangement and though she knew it was in the best interests of you kids that

Michael and I stay Mum, she felt like she was an accomplice to deception and could not hold it in anymore. We spoke together over the phone about keeping such information quiet since you kids were not hurting in any way. However, she may have kept quiet but then after some time as though on cue, she would become agitated about the agreement. That is why you saw her the way you did. She could not even bother to hide it and the rest is history. Here we are".

"So you are saying that we have been raised by the best love in the world. We were loved to death". Ashley walked over to Michael and hugged him saying "Thank you daddy for all that you have done for us. We love you so much and are sorry that we despised you. Will you ever forgive us please"? "No Ashley and Kenroy, it is I who needs your forgiveness. I should have not left you guys to begin with. That was the biggest mistake in my life. I will never do that again. A beloved friend died because of me and so I must make amends. Please forgive me my dear kids ".

There was a knock on the door at that moment and Aunt Sally was ushered in. "I guess you have had a chat with the kids then Michael and Nancy". The look on both their eyes confirmed to Sally her suspicions. Sally went towards the kids and Nancy and the five of them hugged each other in an embrace that was full of love, forgiveness, joy, sorrow and relief all in one. The rest of the years were lived in love and understanding. Kenroy went back to school and graduated with honors. He became one of the most successful music producers in his genre and it was because he did it with passion. Ashley became the head teacher at one of the high schools in her town. She became a respected authority in her field.

She was known all around the world through her books that she wrote that touched mostly on family ties. She continues doing such down to this day. As for Francis and Nancy, they renewed their vows and built a recreational center that they named the Nicholas center for youths. They keep on building such centers around communities so that kids can be taught the values of close knit family ties. Sally passed away a happy woman who lived a long and enjoyful life. The kids always visited her grave twice a year to pay their respects to a woman who made it possible for them to achieve and enjoy what they did. It was an ending that was written in love and passion.

HIS FIRST DAY AT SCHOOL

6 A BLESSING IN BARACK.

He was a very cute bouncing baby boy who was the joy of his father and mother and adored by his sisters. He was so sweet and cute.

As a baby, he was the cutest title boy in the neighborhood. He was a little over seven pounds at birth and was welcomed into the world with lots of love and affection. Mark was his name. Barack Mark.

His father worked at the local high school as a teacher and mentor. He dearly loved his son. When the boy was one year old, his father changed jobs so that he could spend more time during the day with his son. He would fight sleep in order to be with his son. The love that he had for his son was the morning coffee that he needed to keep him awake. Love for a child is the strongest bond that a parent can have for his kids. Mark started walking at exactly one year and one week, about the average amount of time that most kids do in fact start walking. Dad was excited about his Barack walking and it was the cutest thing to see.

Barack loved his father too. That was clearly evident by the way Barack did not want too many people to hold him even if it was his mother sometimes.

He was the spitting image of his father and whenever the three of them, mother father and son could go to the grocery store or just anywhere, people would just give them lovable looks and accolades. The father Prentice never neglected his other children Ashley and Daneisha. He loved Daneisha very much and as a first born, she had a special place for her in his heart. She was always the cute little girl from eternity as his first born.

Ashley was the second in the hierarchy. She was unique in her own way. She was like her father. Conservative and cautious as to who she would befriend. It was a wonderful and beautiful family. What was even more beautiful was the attention that Barack's siblings showered him with and without the faintest of slightest hint of jealousy. The two girls knew that their father would never neglect them. And so it was with the life that the Taylor family lived.

The years went by and Barack turned three. His father's love grew ever so deeper by the day and the two became so close. Barack would go with his father everywhere on every occasion dad had him take him. The two went together one day to buy a PlayStation system and it was like two little boys in the same room. At the age of three, little Barrack was almost an expert in putting together a game system like no other three year old would. Sometimes even mom would become jealous. She however knew everything that was happening was simply the course of nature. She knew that Prentice loved all his kids equally and Barack was a boy and sometimes fathers and sons just have a special kind of relationship in much the same way that mothers and daughters have a special bond.

"Daddy, what are we going to do tomorrow after you come from work? Asked the three year old to his father. Son, we are going to rent a movie you and me and then we can get some ice cream, buy some groceries and cook for the family. Would you like that Barack? "

His son was totally excited as they planned their schedule for tomorrow. Daddy loved to spend time with his kids but Barack had that special place in his heart. Barack and his father were playing basketball on their game console as they spoke together. Mom walked in at that moment and was upset about something. "Is everything okay mom". Barack despite his tender age could sense that there was something wrong with or bothering his mother.

He paused the game and went and hugged his mother as he looked up at her lovingly. His mother looked down at her son and said "I am okay son, I am just very happy and excited that you are my little boy. Sometimes people may look sad when they are actually very happy". That was the reaffirmation that the little boy needed to hear. He did not like to see either of his parents or even siblings unhappy. Barack then went over to his, unpaused the game and both guys gleefully proceeded from where they stopped. Daneisha came in to the room that father and son called their little man cave.

"Dad, you need to fix the window in my room. There is a draught that seeps through especially when it is windy. Please check on it. I do not think I can easily spend one more night in that room". Prentice promised to take care of the situation within the next three hours". Daneisha then went out of the house into the waiting car with her friends. It was Friday evening, spring break and what better thing would a teenage girl prefer than to spend time with her girlfriends.

The two boys played the game for one more hour. It was around three O'clock in the afternoon. It was a lazy day and even Ashley was upstairs watching the television that her father had bought her when she was about the same age as her brother. At around four o'clock, Prentice told his wife that he was heading to the nearest Redbox to return the movie that was three days past due. He was just going to return the movie and also gas up the two vehicles, a habit that he had been practicing for years. A full tank of gas every Friday was enough for the family since they did not drive around too much. They only drove where they needed to drive.

Dad buckled Barack and then got into the driver's seat and headed towards his destination. He waved to two of his friends along the way as he drove. This was a small town and everyone knew everyone, something that a private person like Prentice completely detested. He liked people and knew that no man is an island but sometimes he just needed his private space. Was it too much to ask to only spend time with his family and socialize with friends from time to time and not always?

Dad pulled up by the Redbox. There were three other people in line and so he decided to wait in his car with his baby boy. He treated him like one walking on eggshells. Even when the lights be dissipated, he did not reason that all he had to do was just walk over to the machine and insert it into the opening and press return. But no, he unbuckled him and carried him to the box with him and returned the disc. His child was not a dice to be taken any chance with.

Prentice then went to the gas station and repeated the process. He unbuckled his child, went inside the convenience store and paid for the gas and returned his son to the car seat. He then pumped the gas while he smiled at his son. Life was good for Prentice. What more could a man ask for? He got back inside his truck and drove back towards the house. He saw a different car parked by the kerb that he had never seen before as he pulled up. It was his wife's cousin and she had come to show the new car that she had bought. It was a pretty nice vehicle with no previous owner. She had three kids of her own and the car was very spacious enough to accommodate her family. Barack was unbuckled and he took his little legs to the new vehicle. "Aunt Stella, can I get a ride in your new car?" "Yes Barack, you sure can. Let me talk to your mommy and daddy and see when you can ride with me dear". Barack was glad to hear that and walked inside their house.

Stella and Jennifer, Prentice's wife, spoke with each other outside the house as Prentice and his two other kids kept inside the house. Barack went to the television and turned the cartoon channel. He started watching Barney. It was hilarious and cute looking at the three year old filled with mirth at the purple colored dinosaur. Well at least that was one less thing that daddy had to worry about. As long as they did not let him binge watch cartoons.

Prentice went outside and had just told Ashley to keep an eye on her younger brother as Prentice went outside to join the two women. He walked around the car admiring it. He had a good relationship with his Wife's cousin and knew that the two women were very close. "Good choice of a car Stella. It is spacious enough for you guys. I know that you had mentioned getting a car sometime soon and I guess it was sooner than later".

Stella was happy that she had been approved to get the vehicle. Their old car had just about seen better days and quite frankly it was good riddance. That car had lately started smoking and it backfired once in a while and caused embarrassment to the driver. "So how is Barack doing? I hear he is quite the handful". It seemed that Barack's reputation had preceded him. To say that he was a handful was putting it mildly.

It was more like two handfuls. "Barack is doing fine Stella. He is growing up healthy and right now he is inside watching Barney". Stella laughed. She had a boy who was a year younger than Barack or thereabout. He was a handful in a way and the two little cousins had spent some time together. They were quite a sight to behold.

Barack started going to daycare as his mother had said that he needed to be around kids his age. While Prentice did not want to go along with this idea, it was a good one. He did not think that it made the most sense. He worked at night and so he had all the time in the world with his son and did not have to pay for the daycare. As for kids his age, he was always with the others kids at the playground and so that was association with the kids he needed.

It hurt Prentice to take his son to the daycare. The good thing about it was that the daycare was run by a close family friend. That did little though to alleviate the situation. At least he did not have to worry about the safety of his son. So during the day when Prentice came home from work at seven in the morning, he did not have as much to do as before. He could only prepare the daycare bag with the supplies needed, dropped Daneisha and Ashley of at school and then came back where he took a quick nap but never left the house unless it was an emergency. Prentice also never let his cell phone out of his sight in case he was called by the school or the daycare.

Barack was growing up and his daddy just wanted time to stop. His first son was growing up fast but he was realistic. He knew that one day, he would leave the nest. Such thoughts always made him call the daycare. "How is Barack doing? Is he behaving himself? " . The daycare lady had become accustomed to prentice calling but she understood where he was coming from. When any parent has to abruptly change the way of doing things especially where their child is concerned, it becomes the norm for them to occasionally drop by or call whenever and at whatever time they felt compelled to.

7 BUG JUICE

Barack loved a certain juice that his father always bought for him. He called it bug juice. Why it was called bug juice was a question he always asked himself. The juice came in different colors that anyone could think about. The most important thing was that Barack loved it. Sometimes Prentice could use the juice as an excuse to go visit his son. Dad would always give him that bug juice as a treat and Barack always did what was good.

There was a time in the month of December when Prentice decided that it was time that he acquired a new or used car. He really needed it. So one afternoon, he took his little boy with him and they went to the car dealership. There was a tan four door sedan that seemed spacious enough for his family of four. Daddy eventually procured the vehicle and that night, Barack and Prentice both rode their newly acquired vehicle home.

It was quite the ride. The car rode smoothly but while they were ten miles out, the car meter indicated that they needed to refuel. Barack was seated at the back seat and he was now five, old enough to know that they needed to satisfy the fuel needs of the car. "Son, we will make it. Do not worry. Daddy is here. Nothing is going to happen". In all honesty, Daddy knew that they were going to be okay. He knew from the salesman that once the indicator light went off as a reminder for the driver to refuel, he or she had ten miles before the automobile stopped. However, caution was still needed. The nearest gas station was five miles away and Daddy was going to stop there. And get there they did with an anxious little boy who was rewarded with three little bug juice packs. There was another incident when Daddy had to go pick up his paycheck from one of the restaurants that he had worked in and had been called in to pick up his final paycheck. So he went again with his son. The boy loved the place and daddy rewarded him a well-deserved treat of churros and hot chocolate. It was a cold day and so daddy figured that they would both get away with having some delicious frothy hit chocolate and an equally delicious snack.

Then the day came. The day that most parents look upon with mixed emotions and feelings. It was Barack's first day at school. How would he take it? On that morning, mother and father made sure that they had him dressed in new clothes, a new bag as well as some packed lunch. The parents took him to school with well charged phones because pictures were going to be taken and kept in the memory bank for future reference and reminders. Barack actually was happy to be in school. His first day went even more smoothly than expected.

The new comers were ushered into a huge hall where there were well designed placards with the names of the respective class teachers in various segments of the room. Barack and his parents saw the teacher that their child was assigned to and had him go over and seat behind it together with the other little people in his age group that were to make this first step of a journey that they were going to make in what is called school.

As Barack progressed in school, so did certain behaviors. The school authorities would call and state that he was being too hyper or he was being too inattentive and could not stay in one spot in the classroom. So the calls came and went. Dad was so unhappy with the whole scenario. He knew that the teachers meant well for his son but they were going about it the wrong way. The calls persisted for a long time and one day the parents received a call yet again but from the principal's office. The two parents came and sat down at the principal's office to listen to what has to be said. "Barack is exhibiting behaviors consistent with and characteristic of ADHD children. His attention span is very short by which time he becomes irritable and fidgety. I called the two of you in today to see if perhaps we can reach some kind of solution to helping the young boy". Those words were painful to both father and mother. They loved their now seven year old and wanted to make sure that they do everything in their power to assist him. "Have you considered taking him to a specialist to either confirm or rule out the ADHD?" If he is such a kid, it is not the end of the world. It just means that he had to be helped in a different way".

The situation in front of mom and dad was dire. Any decision that they could make would impact their little boy permanently. "Mrs. Torrance, we will visit a specialist just to see what they will say but we know our son. This is not the boy who we see at home every day ". However, for the well-being of the boy, we shall go see one immediately". And so it was that the following week on his day off from work, Daddy took his only son to a specialist. He somehow felt deep down inside that there was another reason for his son's behavior. The boy who was seated behind the car he was driving was and always was a very calm child. He was playful but what kid is not? That does not mean that he was a bad kid. Actually Barack was a very intelligent kid. The problem he had was more internal and not academic.

Prentice parked his car at the parking lot of the psychologist office that he was going to see. He opened the door with his son in tow and checked in with the front desk receptionist. It was one thirty in the afternoon and their appointment was at one forty. They did not have to wait long. The receptionist invited them to go into the adjacent doorway whereby they were attended to by the Doctor's PDA. "Any allergies, any family history of diabetes...... He crossed out most if not all questions. His son was healthy both mentally and physically and so he did not see the need to even be here in the first place.

"So what seems to be the matter today?" Daddy had something suddenly pop up in his mind but decided that it would be unwise to verbalize it. "The school that my son attends advised us to schedule a visit with Barack in regards to the details described in his file ". The last thing on Prentices mind was to make his son out to be the thing that his teachers thought Barack was and he was not going to verbalize it, least of all in front of his son.

After a few tests were run and performed on Barack by the practitioner specialist, the findings proved to be not what was as expected. "Are you sure you and the teachers....excuse me....the teachers recommend you send your son here? Prentice was wondering why the specialist was asking this question when the recommendation letter was on the latter's table a foot away from his chin on the solid mahogany desk. "That is what the letter in front of you, signed by his class teacher and Principal states. Unless I took a wrong turning somewhere, that is what the letter states Doctor".

The Doctor looked at the letter one more time

and concurred with Prentice. "Mr. Mark, we have a situation here. Your son does not need any kind of help from any specialist. It is his teachers who seriously need all the help they can get". Prentice thought that perhaps he had misheard the teacher. "I am sorry Sir, could you repeat your statement" said Prentice. " I have seen thousands of cases like this where worried parents come in thinking that something is wrong with their child when actually it is the complete opposite. You have a big fish in a small pond. Your son is gifted Prentice. He is highly intelligent and the reason that he is having behaviors is because he is what is psychologically described as being highly sensitive. Most people grow up not realizing this".

Prentice was keenly paying the closest attention to what was being said. He knew that his boy was okay in every sense of the word. "So what now Doctor?". First and foremost, I will arrange to meet with his class teacher and Principal. If they are not informed as soon as possible about the magnitude of Barack's true nature, it would spell disaster"

The Doctor told Prentice to research on the topic of highly sensitive children and adults because this trait of sensory processing sensitivity as it was scientifically called was a boon to the host if identified and a babe if not. "You see Mr. Mark, highly sensitive children are not like other children. One of their key identifiers is the fact that their nervous systems are super active. They become so stimulated when around crowds and that is why they seem to be labelled as overactive or inattentive which brings me to another special characteristic ". Prentice crossed his legs. "Do you have any coffee Doctor?" This was about the most interesting news that he had heard since the invention of sliced bread. "So is there any medication involved?

The Doctor was trained in Europe and the training credentials that lined his walls proved that. He explained further to Prentice that in America, kids were misdiagnosed and wrongly medicated. The kids went through life lifeless intellectually because someone somewhere thought they were helping the child but were instead suppressing genius, creativity and talent.

The kid was then labelled as ADHD or Bipolar

and any deviation from the norm or misbehavior was automatically blamed on his or her condition. What was even worse was that the innocent child grew up thinking that something was wrong with it. That is the worst sentence that can be I posed upon a child. It would be like telling a gifted child that they are less than average. People like Albert Einstein and Torrance Edison were once told by his teacher that "they were "too stupid to learn anything" or in the case of Einstein, The teachers stated that "he was mentally slow" while his parents thought he was "sub-normal ". Well thanks to these "stupid, mentally slow and Sun-normal children" we are literally a light bulb away from the dark ages.

"Thank you Doctor. I am sure this handy information has saved us from making a mistake that would have significantly and negatively changed my child's life for the worst. That evening, there was a small celebration in behalf on the news that has been received. The Principal and the teachers in Barack's school were updated on new methods of coping or dealing with gifted children who would otherwise be mislabeled, pigeonholed wrongly and treated differently because of lack of knowledge.

The worst thing that a parent

would unknowingly do to a highly sensitive child would be to encourage the child to participate in sports activities or activities that stimulate. This children are already naturally stimulated and this is because their minds are constantly thinking. Can you imagine waking up and just finding yourself thinking without even bothering to think. Such children make the best detectives, accountants, writers, artists and even counselors. They are great in careers that are people oriented but in a helping sense. They are great nurses, great care givers as well as great therapists all because they have deep and caring tendencies. They deeply feel the pain and joys of others like it was their own pain.

Can you imagine medicating such people so that these naturally occurring tendencies are inhibited? Society has been hardened and so more caring and tender people are needed. Unfortunately, the very professionals who are counted upon to help bring the balance in the world we live in are the very ones who are frontrunners in advocating that these tender souls be "kept in check"

People need to read more about unique traits in children

and seek second or third opinions of they feel so strongly about and against what they hear. We are given the gift of intuition for a reason. There have been cases of women being told that they could never bared children and as such need to have their ovaries removed but upon second opinion, were encouraged to have two or three more kids safely. Imagine looking up at your teenage son or daughter who is very healthy, loving and full of joy and imagine that you had failed to listen to your gut feeling. That can prick your conscience tremendously.

Avoid listening to scandalous fairy tales because sometimes even with the best of intentions, that is really what they are. Scandalous fairy tales.

BETRAYAL OF TRUTH

8   PUNISHED FOR HARDWORK

The deputy removed the cuffs from the inmate who had spent the night at the jailhouse for the last three days. He had been wrongly convicted by a man he had worked for who without any remote conception of what it means to have facts before having someone arrested, had someone arrested without having any facts.

The innate was dressed in the traditional orange stripped suit that just seemed to undoubtedly tell o lookers one thing. "This person has done something bad. Factually speaking, the inmate had been working at an assisted living facility and was the employee supervisor there. He had faithfully executed his duties for five years.

Prentice joined the nursing program at the Platt Academy for nursing students. He had been a basic entry level nursing assistant for three years and as compared to even his superiors, he had more vision oriented ideas than they did. Nursing seemed to come almost naturally to him and he had decided to go back to school to help better his chances of taking care of his children. It had not been easy joining this nursing program and only the very best were considered. Some prospective students in the past had been turned down five or six times but kept on coming back in the hopes that perhaps next time the powers that be might see things differently. So for Prentice to get an opportunity was his ticket to doing what he passionately loved? Sadly, it seemed that each time something good happened or was about to happen in his life, he seemed to always have domestic issues with his wife.

Two weeks into his program and with a new born baby boy, his wife got into one of her moods and he decided that instead of going back and forth with his wife, he would rather sleep in his car. It was summer time and at around ten o'clock at night, the yelling and shouting started. As he was leaving, his middle finger got caught in the door and the wife slammed it shut and in the process shattered the middle finger. He had it put into a cast and did not let that stop his dreams of obtaining his education. The pain was excruciating. So he was homeless, was not able to see the two daughters and newly born son and now he had to sleep in his car and the summers were very

humid. He sweated like a squeezed sponge but his desire to make

his children's and wife's lives more comfortable kept him going

on.

He would go to school from

Monday through Friday and on Saturdays he would work a double

shift to try and provide for his family. It seemed that at least there

was some sanity at work. He often wondered why he was going

through what he was going through. All he wanted was to take care

of his children. Was there anything so wrong with that? He thought

about his life while parked at the local Walmart parking lot with

the window cracked to cool him down during the night. It was not

at all comfortable but at least no one was shouting at him.

His life went on like this for two weeks when he got his paycheck from his workplace. He managed to get a trailer park house on the outskirts of the town and gladly settled there. He had enough for rent each month but it would not be long before his electricity would be cut off. At least he had a roof over his head. He would sometimes wake up and find a rodent on his chest with its front legs up and just starring at him. He wondered how long it had been there. Had it been watching him sleep? "Why am I even questioning the intention of a rodent? This is a trailer park home. What do you expect? It is not exactly the four seasons.

You get what you pay for. He thought about his warm bed and kids and why he had to pay two bills at two places yet he had done nothing to deserve this. It really took points off his self-esteem. His confidence in himself ebbed at an all-time low.

Prentice arrived home in his four door red sedan. It was a Thursday and he had a rough day at school. He wanted nothing better to do than rest. At the time, the proliferation of cell phones was just commencing. He did not have one to communicate with his children and he sorely missed them. He thought about his daughters Asia and Daneisha and that brought him strength to keep on struggling. With the arrival of his son Balak, he only got strengthened even more. He would even sleep outside in crazy humidity and the thoughts of his children would cool him down.

That following day, he went to school as usual and was pleasantly surprised to find out that he was the student of the phase. That meant that he would get the best parking spot for a week and a one hundred dollar gratuity for his work. If only he could get a reward for taking care of his kids. That afternoon, he left school as usual and headed to the trailer park. He arrived at his trailer at around eight in the evening. He unlocked the door and with his fingers pushed up the light switch as he always did on each occasion at dusk or dawn. The lights had been disconnected for failure to pay. His wife had taken him to court for child support and as such he was hemorrhaging his hard earned funds towards the upkeep of his children. He was so mentally exhausted that he did not care about the heat, rodents whatever else was lurking. He had to finish school come rain or high water.

He actually slept well that night and on Saturday morning, he went to see his children before he went to work. He arrived at his old apartment and found the wife and kids watching cartoons and just spending time together. He walked in and his daughters jumped up in excitement when they beheld him. They started asking him why he left and that question caught him unawares. How does a victim of emotional abuse answer such a question? It was Prentices wife who was making him look like the deserter. Talk about adding insult to injury. It was too painful for him to bear. He tactfully diverted their attention from the question using the time tested question that always worked. "Who wants to go get some ice cream with Daddy?" That was enough even to arouse the baby Balk.

This moment was the highlight of his week. Anything that he had done wrong did not matter at this particular moment. Nothing mattered at the moment. The nights he spent sleeping inside his car on hot summer nights, the nights he slept in his trailer park home without electricity with a fearless rodent and a throbbing middle finger. It was like the relief a hitherto expectant mother goes through in the stages of childbirth until the arrival of the child and all she sees and experiences is the joy she gets when she sees the infant. He took the kids to the ice cream shop and they are the best

I've cream they ever had. It seemed to taste better when Daddy and mommy or either of them went with them.

Prentice took the kids to the park where they laughed and jumped and played for about ninety minutes before Prentice decided that it was best that they go back inside the shade. The kids were not too happy to see their father leave but they understood that their father had to go to work to be able to pay for their upkeep.

Prentice went to work and he was entrusted with the funds to buy the clients at the assisted living center anything that they needed and not necessarily wanted. On this day, one of the clients was stating that he was bored and needed a television in his room. Prentice initially encouraged the client to go to the main lobby and watch the big fifty eight inch television that the other clients all watched despite having their own televisions.

Janny was not in a listening mood. He started ranting and raving and kicking and screaming. He had the funds in his account and knew his rights. Prentice was not in a mood to engage in any verbal exchanges with anyone least of all the clients he had been entrusted to take care of.

"Okay Janny, let us go and see if we can procure a television for you. It is your money and I cannot stop you from what you desire. Those few words brought a different expression of gratitude relief and exhilaration in Janny's face that Prentice gladly welcomed. It was five o'clock and it was dinner time. Janny munched away at his baby back ribs, a treat they got every Saturday. Janny was having a ball .Everything he desired he was getting. Very soon he could claim proud ownership of a television set.

Prentice loaded the company van with three of the clients as stipulated by official company policy so that it is counted as an official trip. He took that two other less demanding clients and one hour and half a gallon of ice cream later, four people arrived back at the assisted living facility.

Prentice parked the company van in reverse and his first priority was the safety and well-being of the clients. He came out and opened the back seat and proceeded to let all four out and paid particular attention to old geyser as he was not nicknamed though in reality his name was Jonathan. Jonathan was lame on one leg and had to be assisted. He took old geyser's hand and helped him disembark whereby he walked by himself into the facility.

It was around eight in the evening and the sun was yet up. Prentice requested one of the other male staff to assist in getting the television down from the van. An hour later after programming the television and all, Janny day down on his recliner that had by all aspects, seen better days. The client was simply in his own little world. Nothing wrong with that. At least the television would keep him out of trouble. Prentice they did his rounds every hour while leaving the other employees to conduct their assigned duties. He never liked to hoover over anyone because he most certainly did not want anyone hoovering over him unless the person was incompetent.

At eleven o'clock, there was the shift change. Prentice had to make sure that the medication count was accurate and that the necessary paperwork was complete. The very last thing that anyone needed was a miscount of psychotropic medication. After everything checked out and a consensus was reached, it was time for Prentice to head out and leave. But where was he going. All that awaited him was a little needy rodent and a trailer that was hotter than a sauna and he was in no need for any exfoliation at the moment. As the Supervisor, he decided to stay on for the next eight hours but keep his distance from the grave yard shift crew. He may be the Supervisor but He was not The Administrator. He could not just do anything he pleased. He spoke to the night nurse and told her that they had cut off his electricity yesterday on the Friday past and could not be back until Monday. He did not give the specifics of how he landed in that situation. That was not information that concerned anyone. They just needed to know enough to be assuaged of his presence.

9   TOUGHNESS DECIDED

The night went by fast. Sunday mornings were a favorite of Prentice as he would now either go for his religious obligations or he would go to the park with his children and play some basketball with his son and daughters or whatever other recreational activity that the kids may like. He clocked out at exactly seven in the morning and proceeded to the park. He thought about his parents. He thought about his childhood and how he could tend to the flock that they owned. He thought about the days when he was in high school and how the principal would tell them during the assembly every Friday that "no education no love".

Prentice did not think much of those words right then but now he saw how important they were. Education did not mean anything at this particular moment. The best education, whatever that meant, could not alleviate his current predicament.

He pulled up by the sandpit that was a favorite of kids at the playground in the park, got out of his vehicle and went and sat at on one of the benches. It was a little after eight in the morning. He thought about school, his kids, his past and the rodent that was in his trailer. "Life". That was a four letter word that had more meaning to it than anything he could think of. He had done everything the right way and sometimes just could not fathom why some things happened the way they did.

"Hallo Prentice. I have not seen you in a long time. What are you doing here so early in the morning?" It was a familiar voice. He already vividly put a face to the sound that uttered it. "IIi Stacy. I scc that you have not changed one bit. You are still every bit the health nut that you always were". The beautiful young woman came and sat down next to him. "You look well prentice. How are the kids? Prentice turned to look at her. He smiled. He smiled and thought. "Life of Life"

"Prentice, did you understand what the Professor was saying in class. I thought he was talking way too fast and especially when it was important material and should have slowed down". "Maybe if you had not partied hard with your girlfriends last night you could be more focused. Do you even know what day it is? ".

The two twenty year olds had known each other since the time they were half their ages and by all means were high school sweethearts. They had been through so much together and the people who knew Prentice and Stacy could say that there was no way these two kids would be anything other than husband and wife.

"Hi Stacy. How was your morning run? At least it is better than a morning hangover and trying to understand accounting principles. "That is not fair Prentice. We were young and stupid. You yourself was not exactly Mr. Perfect you know"

"Ah life" thought Prentice to himself as memories flooded from the past regarding him and this now still young looking woman who though in her mind thirties as was Prentice, looked only a day older than twenty one. "I am just sited and relaxing watching the sunrise". Prentice said that with an air of indifference like one who had to think of what to say quickly after being caught red handed inside the cookie jar. Stacy had been through a very tough and bitter divorce with a man who had misrepresented himself as someone he was not. He had been verbally abusive to Stacy and had it not been for the kids, she could have left him much sooner. She had thought that he could have a change of heart and become a better man but that was really wishful thinking. A wolf Wil always be a wolf even if it puts on the best sheep make-up. He beat her down at every turn. He would demean her in front of her grinds, in front of her family and even her daughter who resented her father like a tick on a healthy cow with her dad being the tick. Everyone who met him left with the same contemptuous attitude and looked at Stacy with piety. Piety.

Piety. It was indeed a religious experience. "You look well Stacy. I guess I should also start running". "That beats looking at a mouse on your chest" he thought.

"Prentice, I did not know that you could cook. All this time I thought that you were just another boyfriend that my Stacy had picked up". Prentice looked up and smiled at the kind hearted woman who was mixing the ground beef and the other ingredients necessary to make meatloaf. She was the mother to the girl he had met five years ago and now at the age of fifteen, he had endeared himself to the parents of Stacy Dad. Her parents owned a local pub and sometimes Prentice could go there just to get some liquid courage. He was not an alcoholic by any stretch of the imagination. He just wanted to temporarily escape the stress around him. He looked at the woman next to him but carefully guarded his heart. The woman seated next to him would have easily been his wife.

He asked himself how it came about that she ended up being with a very abusive man instead of him but stopped himself. Looking back in the past to what could have been was pointless. The past had its's memories and that was all that it could offer. He was a married man now and he was not the type to do anything foolish like covet another woman while he was still married regardless of whether there was stability in the marriage or not

10 GOOD THINGS FOR THE PATIENT.

Prentice and Stacy sat in silence and it was like they were both thinking about memories that would not benefit neither at the moment. Were there any regrets? Perhaps a few but that was in the past. The elephant was in the room and they both did not want to see it.

"We can both sit here and stare at the sand pit or we can say what we both want to say. We do not even have to be mined readers". "I have been trying to get a hold of you Prentice and I heard from the grapevine that you are not with your wife currently. You even shattered your finger. We both have or at least had a spouse who abused us and it was not all sunshine and lollipops Prentice but we had to make do with what we had.

Prentice loved his wife but there was no hiding his past with Stacy. They had shared so much together in the past and everyone had already believed that they were headed for marriage. Prentice had told his current wife about Stacy. He had to. It was part of the dating process where you have to tell your future spouse to be about your past so that they can make a judgement as to whether they should proceed or not. It was only fair that the other person know your details in case you were the axe murderer.

Stacy and Prentice began to study together and do most things together under a good chaperone of course. They were both in the debating club at school as well as the drama club. Their teachers adored them and the rest of the students held them in high esteem. "This is for you. You deserve only the best Stacy" said

Prentice as he handed Stacy a neatly wrapped package. Stacy unwrapped it and her eyes became wide opened beaming with not as she saw what Prentice had given her. It was a golden necklace with two diamond stones and a pair of matching earrings. "She hugged Prentice.

"Thank you so much Prentice. I love it". Turn around Stacy. He took the necklace and carefully and gently secured it around his beloved Stacy's neck. She would have to put on the earrings later.

"Now I feel guilty that I have not gotten anything for you Prentice ". Prentice looked at Stacy with a love filled heart. "Stacy, each time I see you, I am getting a present and unwrapping it. You are all the present I need". Stacy was attracted to Prentice for this very reason. He spoke from his heart. Prentice later that Wednesday evening went home a very happy young man knowing that he had made this one special girl very happy by offering her

this wonderful friendship gift and even more so because she had

gladly accepted it. He called her.

"Hi Stacy. I was just calling to make sure that you

had arrived home well from your little sister's concert". "Hi

Prentice, we just arrived like fifteen minutes ago and Madeline

sang very well. She received the second prize. She was not too

happy but given the nature of the talent, anyone in the top five was

like first position.

Prentice got up and looked at Stacy. Being with her was fun

but never to face reality. Things were different now and he was in

a very difficult situation at the moment. "Here is the key to my

Father's old house. No one stays there but I have decided to sleep it

and maintain it. I do not want to sell it.

There may be an emergency and I may need it. Right now you seem to need it more than I do Prentice. If it makes you feel better, I will never drop by to check up on you. We don't want any raised eyebrows. Prentice, this is simply about being human. If I were a man, I could do the same thing. Do not let your pride tell you no. You cannot function well with inadequate rest".

Prentice took the keys and looked long and hard at Stacy. "Thank you Stacy. I must go now. Thank you so much". Stacy watched him leave and went for a stroll along the park's strolling trails. Prentice drove over to the house where Stacy's late father lived. This was the house where she had been raised. It was the house where he had come as a little boy and played with the woman who had just handed him the keys to the house when they were age mate's years ago. Prentice was tired. He had slept on one of the lobby chairs at work. The sleep was okay. It beat sleeping in what he called his oven. Prentice unlocked the door and what a sight met his eyes. The house was immaculate.

Stacy definitely had kept her word of maintaining it. Anyone would want to stay here. Then place was clean. He walked over to the kitchen and it was even better. He had cooked here before and the fridge that he had put his jello mixture to solidify was still in use. He smiled. Good memories. He went to the pantry to see if he needed to restock it as a sign of gratitude to Stacy with the little funds he had on him and upon opening the door, he got quite the surprise. The pantry had enough to feed a small army. There were cans of bean, pea, spinach that could expire in the next millennium and there were lots of soups, rice as well as onions and other food items that he could survive on for a few days until he got his situation straightened out.

He walked over to the room where he had spent the night years ago on the invitation of Stacy's mother. The bed was not the same one but everything else in the room had been left intact. Even the color of the room was still the same. Even after twenty years, no one can forget a bright red room. He smiled to himself.

He went back to his car and got his little travelling suitcase. It had enough for a week's change of clothes. Prentice threw the suitcase on the bed he was going to sleep on tonight and took out his towel and other toiletries. He took a slow warm shower and after changing our of his dress clothes, donned his pajamas and got inside the covers and was soon in dreamland.

Prentice stirred. It was four o'clock in the afternoon. He had slept for six straight hours and he felt refreshed. He was more tired than he thought. His mind went back to the past.

"Prentice, could you please come and help me cut the onions" said Melissa, Stacy's mother. Melissa was preparing meatloaf, a favorite of her husband as well as Prentice. "Please dice them as we want their flavor in the meat loaf without the chunks of onion". Melissa was a good cook and knew what she was talking about. It was a Friday evening and it was a special occasion. Stacy had just won the regional spelling bee competition and had received an all bills paid trip to New York City for one weekend with any three people whom she wanted.

The three were a no brainer. Her and her parents but since her father had previous work related obligations, he was unable to accompany them even after pleading to his employer to temporarily get someone to work in his place. Prentice felt thirsty and went to the silver fridge that had all kinds of drinks that one could imagine. Orange juice, grape juice, chicken soup as well as mango nectar for Stacy's father who was a health nut.

He grabbed the orange juice bottle that was partially opened and emptied the contents into a plastic cup and drank away. "The way you are drinking makes it seem like their will be no more orange juice after today Prentice. You must be extra a thirsty today ". Stacy had near crept up and startled him. He did not hear her walk into the kitchen. "Stacy, congratulations on your success. More importantly, thank you for inviting me. I was humbled by the opportunity to go in place of your father ".Stacy looked at Prentice and smiled. "I could not think of anyone better suited to take his place".

Flashbacks were replaced by a knock on the front door. He opened the door to find Stacy weeping. "Stacy, are you alright? Tell me what is wrong". He led her to the living room and they both sat down on the two chaise lounge that her father had bought at a furniture store years ago and looked immaculate.

"Prentice, why are we pretending like this? Maybe you can do it easily but I cannot. We both have spouses that despise us yet we still stay with them. Does not what we have been through together mean anything to you? Prentice was like one who had been sucked punched. He did not know what hit him. "Stacy that part of our past has no place in our present". Prentice was married and he was not going to do anything to jeopardize that situation. The mere fact that he was alone with this beautiful woman in the living room made him very uncomfortable. This two age mates had grown up together and were joined at the hip. They had also spoken about marriage right before they had turned twenty. Yet here they were in the present.

Prentice and his wife were apart. He wondered why such things were befalling him. He missed his kids. Here was a woman who loved him and with who they shared a very close past. "Stacy I feel that if we are to talk, let us meet in a public place and not here. That way everything we say to each other does not lead to any unfortunate happenings and we feel guilty later on. "As had as that is Prentice, my respect for you has me agree with you"

Years later, Prentice and his wife dissolved their union. It was very difficult and it hit Prentice so hard. Even after the dissolution, he still tried his best to make it work but that was not to be.

"I guess all good things come to those who wait". Prentice looked at his bride as they got into their vehicle and on their way to their honeymoon. "Prentice dear, I left you waiting for me at our wedding and disappeared for three years and when I came back, you were already taken. I was so mad at myself and wed someone else out of the rebound. I will never leave you again"

Sometimes life can be puzzling and the couple learnt a lesson that made them wiser and their relationship stronger. Prentice drove out into the sunset with his Stacy by his side. Theirs was a cruise ship about to take off for in an hour and they had booked a long week trip on it.

ABOUT THE AUTHOR

GEORGE Okora is a Kenyan Author who writes truth based books

in narrative form to enable the readers to relate to the characters

therein and apply the entire situation of each of the characters in their own life.